THE PINK LADY

Celebrating Life Journey of Sabeen Mansoor through Food

Written by: Sabeen's Family

MAPLE
PUBLISHERS

The Pink Lady – Celebrating Life Journey of Sabeen Mansoor through Food

Author: Sabeen's Family

First Published in 2021

ISBN: 978-1-914366-69-7 (Paperback)
  978-1-914366-67-3 (Hardback)
  978-1-914366-68-0 (Ebook)

Book cover design, Illustrations and Book layout by:

  Professional Designer, Sabeen's Friends and Family

Published by:
  Maple Publishers
  1 Brunel Way,
  Slough,
  SL1 1FQ, UK
  www.maplepublishers.com

A CIP catalogue record for this title is available from the British Library.

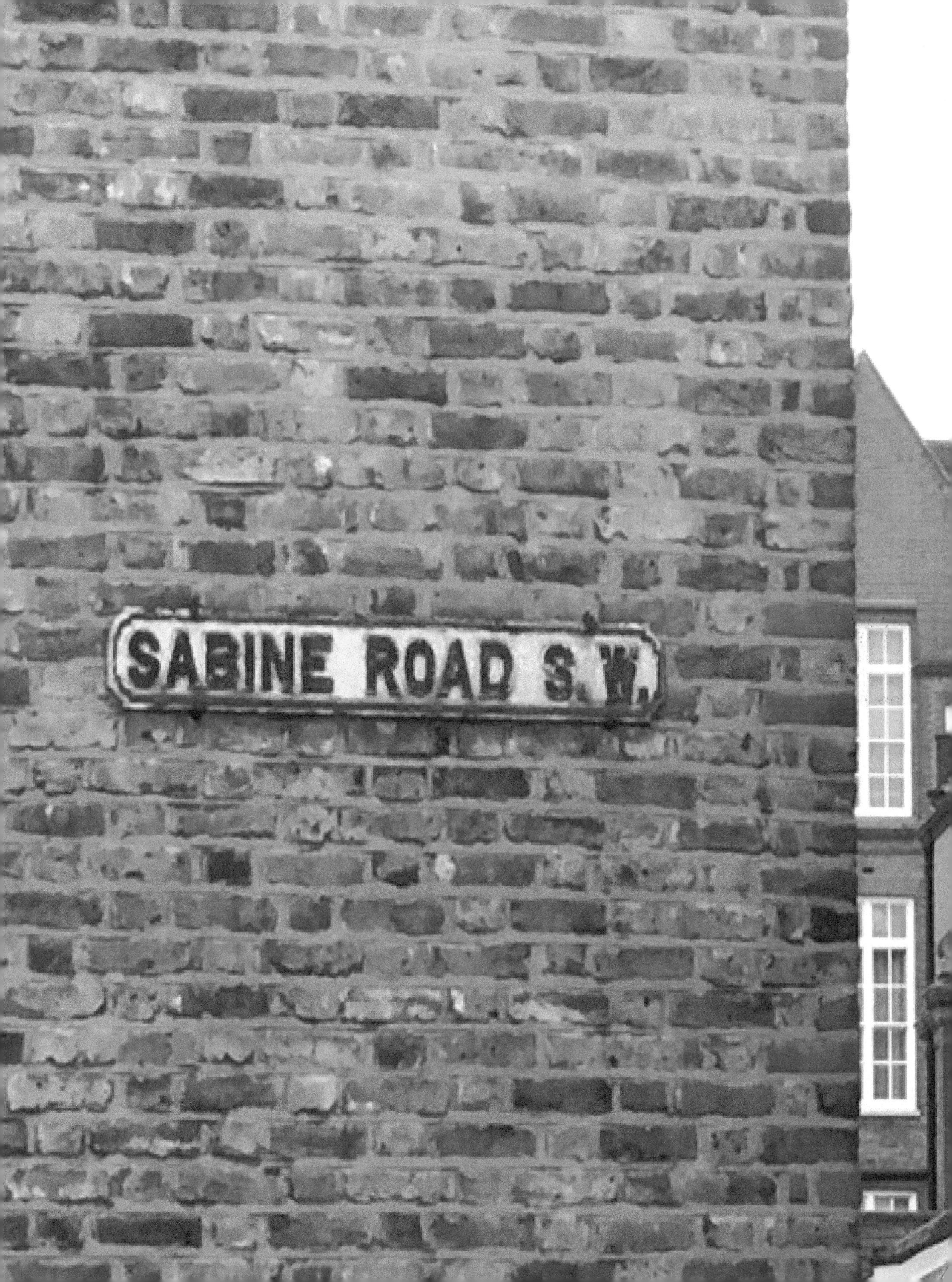
SABINE ROAD S.W.

IN LOVING MEMORY OF

SABEEN MANSOOR
FOREWORD

As we write this foreword, we find ourselves in emotional overdrive. Sabeen left us on February 24, 2021, to meet our Creator due to the awful Covid-19 pandemic. Never in our wildest dreams did we think that such a beautiful, pure, innocent, talented, and loved person could go so early; she was just 43!

Our life without her is incomplete.

In our small family of 4 people (including our cat Sky), Sabeen was always the centre of attention. All of us were in love with her. We hovered around her to seek her opinion, protect her from harm, and make her as happy as we could. Her desires became our passions; our son (Sameer) and I felt so glad to make her happy.

Once Sabeen and Sameer went to the House of Fraser. Sabeen liked a mobile phone cover with the iconic Swarovski Swan design on the back but decided not to buy it that day. Later that day, Sameer went with his friends and bought it for her with his pocket money as a Mother's Day gift. She was deeply touched that he remembered and hugged him.

In addition to being a loving mother and the best wife one could ever have, Sabeen was also an amazing cook and a very successful businesswoman running her Food Services and Catering business in London called **Pink Oven**. She built it from scratch to the heights of success in just three years. She was very kind and attentive to her clients, sometimes even advising them on things beyond food – they all loved her and affectionately called her **The Pink Lady**.

We have compiled this book to honour her life, passion for Pakistani cuisine, and her compassion for people. It includes a collection of her most delicious and sumptuous recipes, organised by the various phases of her life journey.

All the key headings are in Sabeen's handwriting, which we were able to preserve digitally, adding a personal touch.

30% of profits from the sale of this book will go to various charities in the UK and Pakistan.

We would love to hear from you about your feelings and feedback about this book. Please get in touch on: welovesabeen@gmail.com.

Sabeen's Family

ACKNOWLEDGEMENT

We would like to thank our family and friends for working passionately to make this book possible.

WE LOVE SABEEN.

CONTENTS
Life is a journey

3 **Singapore**
Family life
Parenthood and Travel

2 **Dubai**
Married life
A baby and a cat

1 **Karachi, Pakistan**
Early life
What a Prankster
Our Love Story

LET US MAKE YOU COMFORTABLE

Although born in Pakistan, Sabeen considered herself an international citizen. Her father was in the Airline industry, so she travelled across many countries in her lifetime. Even after we got married, we had the opportunity to live and work on three different continents. This greatly influenced how Sabeen crafted her skills as a chef and business owner. She would easily make South-East Asian, Western, and Pakistani cuisine all in one cooking session.

Here we list all the essential ingredients Sabeen uses in her recipes. Many of the herbs and spices are typically used in Pakistani cooking, which is the influence for many of the dishes in this book.

1. Poppy Seeds
2. Javatri (Ground Mace)
3. Jaifal (Ground Nutmeg)
4. Kashmiri Red Chilli (Whole)
5. Kasoori Methi (Dried Fenugreek)
6. Haldi (Turmeric)
7. Kashmiri Red Chilli Powder
8. Red Chilli Powder
9. Bay Leaf
10. Ground Red Chilli Flakes
11. Garam Masala Powder
12. Coriander Seeds
13. Black Pepper Powder
14. Curry Leaves
15. Fennel Seeds
16. Cumin Powder
17. Cardamom Pods
18. Cinnamon Powder
19. Salt
20. Dried Lemon
21. Whole Red Chilli
22. Coriander Powder
23. Cumin Seeds
24. White Pepper Powder
25. Cinnamon Sticks

Useful Techniques and Terminologies

Along with the essential spices, it is also important to understand the authentic methods of cooking Pakistani cuisine. Traditional cookbooks may not include these details since they come naturally to writers from the local culture. We would like everyone to have the confidence to prepare Sabeen's dishes by knowing all there is to know how to produce an authentic Pakistani dish. Below we list some key techniques and terminologies that will help you to produce original dishes in the right culinary context.

Pakistani Curry Base:

A certain level of consistency and colour is needed to make an authentic curry. The base of any Pakistani curry starts by frying chopped onions in hot oil until they turn golden-brown. This is then followed by adding ginger garlic paste and a little water to achieve the final curry base. This technique is the start of most curry dishes and must be perfected to achieve the perfect curry consistency.

Bhono:

This is a very common term in Pakistani cooking. When someone says "Bhono", it refers to the process of removing the smell from meat and ensuring that masala is cooked. This is achieved by moving your spoon clockwise in half circles and always ending towards the middle of the pot till the oil separates.

Tarka:

Tarka is infused oil (you can use sunflower oil or ghee) that is poured over a finished dish (such as Daal or Haleem – see pages 194 and 154), bringing extra taste and flavour. You start by heating the oil and then adding Cumin Seeds, Curry Leaves, Dried Red Chillies, Chopped Garlic, or Ginger (you can also put fewer ingredients if you prefer). Fry the herbs or spices for 2-3 minutes in the hot oil and then pour onto the finished dish. This will always make a sizzling sound owing to the hot oil.

Brown the onion:

This is a critical step in curry making and helps achieve a dark colour. It's important that you don't burn the onion. Otherwise, the curry will taste bitter.

1 Kanee:

This is a very important term when cooking rice in Pakistani households! During the process of boiling rice, there comes a stage when you can press the rice grains between your thumb and index fingers and the grains break into two. This means that "1 Kanee" has been achieved and tells you that the rice is ready to be drained and put on "Dum".

Dum:

Dum is a process that creates perfect, fluffy rice. It is a slow process that involves steaming rice on low heat until it is completely cooked and a fluffy texture is achieved. Once 1 Kanee has been achieved, the rice should be put on "dum" for 5-10 minutes maximum to finish. Note that over-steaming will make the rice texture mushy, so it's key to get this part right!

Papar (Papadum):

Papar is a round wafer made with various doughs, spices, and herbs. They are usually eaten with a main meal like Daal and Rice.

Whole Garam Masala:

Another staple in Pakistani cuisine that provides a unique taste and an inviting aroma to the final dish. It can also be used as a garnish when sprinkled over a finished dish. Whole Garam Masala is made by grinding Bay Leaves, Cinnamon, Star Anise, Cloves, Black Pepper Corns, Coriander Seeds, Cumin Seeds, Fennel Seeds, and Cardamom.

Papri:

This is essentially a deep-fried cracker made from flour. They are usually used as a garnish for extra crunchy mouthfeel when having Chana Chaat (see page 62) or Dahi Baray (see page 64). These are readily available in any ethnic Pakistani food shop.

Desi:

This is very common terminology among Pakistani diasporas. This refers to the items coming from the wider region of Pakistan and India. These can be food, clothes, shoes, etc.

Pakistani Chinese:

It's the terminology used to describe the Pakistani taste adaptation of Chinese cuisine.

EARLY DAYS

Sabeen began her early life in Karachi, Pakistan.

She was born on March 9, 1977, into a well-educated and well-off family, to parents Shahid Hassan Khan and Shahnaz Khan. Her birthday remained very important for her throughout her life, and if someone forgot it, then all hell broke loose! Every year in January, she would start reminding her best friend (who had the same name as her) that she better not forget to wish her well that year.

Her late father was an Aeronautical Engineer in the PIA and studied in Scotland while her mother studied in England. After studying, her mother worked for a paint company in Karachi. Sabeen spent most of her childhood in CP Berar Housing Society, where she spent unforgettable days playing with her cousins and playing pranks on people. Sabeen was well travelled and had visited many countries around the world, including as far away as the US and Japan.

From an early age, she was a naughty child and was dearly loved by her family. Her elder sister, Umbreen (who Sabeen called Apa out of respect and who now lives in the US with her husband and two sons), was quite protective of her and used to fight with the girl at school who bullied Sabeen. Once when Sabeen was four months old, Umbreen spotted a lizard. She quickly picked her up and ran to their mother without realising that Sabeen was just a few months old and needed to be held from the back of her head to keep her neck steady. She was screaming about the lizard while their mother was scolding Umbreen for not picking her correctly. Such was Umbreen's love for her younger sister.

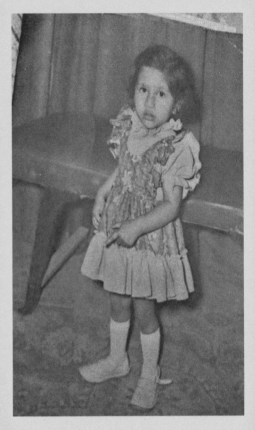

Sabeen was very shy and always avoided confrontation. Throughout her life, people stood up for her because she would not. I would always make sure that she felt protected when out and about and have given many people a piece of my mind if they were mean to her! This was on buses, roads, and even at Disneyland Paris! I just didn't want anyone to disrespect her, as I knew that she would not fight back. She was simple and innocent, which is very rare to find in the world we live in today! This is the most attractive thing about her that convinced me to spend the rest of my life with her.

Once out of the CP Berar house, her family settled in the KDA Officers Society, which is behind the National Cricket Stadium in Karachi. It remains their house today and the place where she spent her adult life until we got married. This is where Sabeen cultivated her love for cats, and at one time, they had 15! Most of them were Siamese, two of which came to Dubai, which is where we moved right after our marriage. It was her condition to join me! I had to concede because nothing was more important to me than having her by my side.

Her early education was at Mama Parsi School, a prestigious girl's school in Karachi, followed by Commerce College. Her friends came from all segments of society as she believed in true friendships rather than how rich or poor someone was. She used to go on the public bus with one of her friends to visit their house, so her friend didn't feel bad, and her driver used to follow them. This compassion for others remained part of her values, which she passed on to our son: "feet on the ground" and "never be proud". The only thing she was proud of was the relationships she had cultivated over time. Today, this is why her family, friends, and even people she only knew over social media, remain upset and deeply shocked about her tragic departure.

To begin this book – a culinary journey through Sabeen's life - we will start with some recipes that Sabeen loved having while growing up.

Mini Margherita Pizza

SNACK

This was one of Sabeen's favourite snacks and an important part of her party menus. These mini delights are a perfect appetiser or snack for your guests and specifically for children. They are very easy to make, but you must get the dough right!

INGREDIENTS

Pizza Dough:
- 3 cups Flour
- 1 tbsp Sugar
- 1 tbsp Salt
- 1 cup Warm Milk
- 2 tbsp Olive Oil
- 2 tsp Yeast
- ½ cup Milk for kneading

Pizza Topping:
- 1½ cup Pizza Sauce
- 2 cups Mozzarella Cheese
- 2 cups Cheddar Cheese
- 2 cups Black Olives
- 1 tsp Mixed Herbs

 Serves:
2-3 Person

 Prep Time:
35-40 minutes

METHOD

- Add warm milk, yeast, and sugar. Mix it all together in a large bowl and leave it for 1 hour till yeast floats to the top.
- Transfer them to a bowl that contains flour, salt, and olive oil. Mix them well together.
- While mixing and kneading the pizza dough, using your hand, add 1/4 cup of milk. If the texture of the dough is still dry, add another ¼ cup of milk until the texture of the dough is soft and fluffy.
- Cover the dough with a towel and leave it for 2 hours.
- Now take a baking tray, grease it with oil and start making the dough into a small round tiny pizza using your hands.
- Brush the dough with oil and then add pizza sauce.
- Next, add toppings and then lastly add cheese. Preheat the oven for 10 mins at 180-degree Celsius.
- Transfer the tray to the oven and cook for 10 mins.

Sabeen Secrets:

- Getting the dough right is the most important part of this dish. Else Pizza will turn out chewy and flat. You want them raised and soft.
- Mixing different cheese enhances the flavour.

Aloo Keema

MAIN

A hearty and comforting dish that Pakistani households regularly have for dinner or lunch. It was a favourite for our son, who prefers it with Sabeen's Special Tarka Daal (see page 194). The aroma of the dish is enhanced by Cinnamon sticks and Garam Masala.

 Serves:
2-3 Person

 Prep Time:
45-50 minutes

 Spice Level:
Medium

INGREDIENTS

- 1 kg Lamb Mince
- 3 Onions (Medium chopped)
- 2 Medium Potatoes (Medium chopped)
- 4 Tomatoes (Medium chopped)
- 1½ tsp Ginger Garlic Paste
- 1 tsp Salt
- 1 tsp Red Chilli
- 3-4 Long Dried Red Chilli
- 1 tsp Cracked Black Pepper (Grind fresh in the grinder but keep course)
- 1½ tsp Coriander Powder
- 1 tsp Cumin Powder
- ½ tsp Turmeric Powder (Haldi)
- ¼ tsp Garam Masala Powder
- 2 Cinnamon Sticks
- 1 Bay Leaf
- Chopped Coriander
- 4 Green Chilies (Whole)
- 3-4 tbsp Sunflower Oil
- 1 tsp Ghee

METHOD

- Heat oil and ghee in a pot.
- Add onions and fry till light brown.
- Add mincemeat, tomatoes, and ginger garlic paste. Bhono.
- Cover the lid and reduce heat for 7 minutes so tomatoes can become soft.
- Add all spices (except garam masala), dried red chilli and bhono, adding a little water in intervals. This will stop spices from burning.
- Once the smell of meat is gone, add 3-4 glasses of water and cook on medium heat for 25-30 minutes so that meat is cooked through. Halfway add potatoes so that these can be cooked.
- Once the meat is cooked, and oil separates, add green chillies and garam masala. Leave 5 minutes to cook.
- Add chopped coriander on top to present a colourful dish.

Sabeen Secrets:

- Don't chop the potatoes too small.
- Don't overcook the potatoes; else, it will become a mash.
- Don't wash the mincemeat.

Chicken Kofta Curry

MAIN

A firm favourite of our son, Sameer. A dish that he could eat every day while we were not so keen that frequently! You can also make it with lamb mince.

Serves:
2-3 Person

Prep Time:
1 hour

Spice Level:
Medium

INGREDIENTS

For Kofta Balls:

- 1 kg Chicken Mince
- 1 Onion (Blended)
- 1 tsp Red Chilli
- 1 tsp Salt
- ½ tsp Turmeric Powder (Haldi)
- ½ tsp Cracked Black Pepper (Grind fresh in the grinder but keep course)
- 1 tsp Ginger Garlic Paste
- 1 Slice of Bread (Soaked in water and broken into pieces)
- 1½ tsp Gram Flour

For Gravy:

- 4-5 Onions (Finely chopped)
- 2 Tomatoes (Chopped)
- 1 tsp Black Pepper Powder
- ½ tsp Garam Masala Powder
- 1½ tsp Kashmiri Red Chilli
- ½ tsp Turmeric Powder (Haldi)
- 1½ tsp Coriander Powder
- 1½ tsp Ginger Garlic Paste
- 1 tsp Cumin Powder
- 1 tsp Red Chilli Flakes
- 1 tsp Dried Fenugreek Leaves

- 1 cup Yoghurt (Whisked and mix 1 tbsp Qorma Masala in this. This is a family secret of having the most delicious Kofta Curry)
- 5-6 Green Chillies Whole
- 1 Coriander Bundle (Chopped)
- Finely Chopped Ginger
- Chopped Green Chillies
- 3-4 tbsp Sunflower Oil
- 1 tbsp Ghee

METHOD

- For Kofta Balls, add all spices, soak bread and onion in minced meat and use your hands to mix it together (you can also grind it). If mixing with hands, it's very important that you put some oil in your hands, so the minced meat does stick in your hands.
- Once done, apply yoghurt in your palms and make equal size Kofta balls to keep aside.
- Now for gravy, add oil and ghee in a pot. Once hot, brown the grounded onions (make sure you don't burn these, onions should be golden brown, not dark brown) and then add ginger garlic paste with a little water. Bhono.
- Add tomatoes, all spices (except fenugreek & garam masala), and bhono till tomatoes are soft. Add some water and leave for 5-7 minutes so that tomatoes are well cooked and mixed into the gravy.
- Then add whisked yoghurt and green chillies into the gravy and bhono.
- Now fry Koftas on the frying pan for 10 minutes and then add it into the gravy to mix. Also, add fenugreek, garam masala powder at this stage.
- Add 1-2 glasses of water and cover the pot to cook.
- Add chopped coriander, green chillies, finely chopped ginger on top to serve.

Sabeen Secrets:

- Don't stir the Koftas with cooking utensil but rather shake the pot to mix well and turn the Koftas.

Egg Fried Rice

MAIN

This was a staple in Sabeen's Pakistani Chinese cuisine. The main difference is the simplicity of ingredients yet including Chinese sauces to enrich the taste profile.

INGREDIENTS

- ½ cup Spring Onions (Chopped)
- 1 cup Carrots (Thinly sliced)
- 1 cup Capsicum (Thinly sliced)
- 1 cup Cabbage (Thinly sliced)
- ½ kg Rice (Boiled)
- 1 tsp Salt
- 3-4 Garlic Cloves (Chopped)
- 1 tsp Black Pepper
- ½ tsp White Pepper
- 3-4 Eggs
- ½ tsp Yellow Food Colour
- 4 tbsp Sunflower Oil
- 2 tbsp Soy Sauce
- 1 tbsp Vinegar

Serves:
4-5 Person

Prep Time:
45-50 minutes

Spice Level:
Low

METHOD

- In a wok, add 2 tbsp oil, eggs and yellow food colour and mix it well. Keep it aside.
- In the same wok, add 2 tbsp oil add garlic and cook it for 2 minutes. Then add carrots and capsicum and mix well. Add cabbage and stir fry all the vegetables for 2-3 minutes on medium to high flame.
- Now add salt, black pepper, white pepper, vinegar and soy sauce and mix well.
- Now add boiled rice, spring onions and fried eggs and toss it well.
- Garnish with spring onion and serve.

Sabeen Secrets:

- When tossing the rice, keep the heat medium; else, rice can burn.
- The egg should be coarsely broken when cooking to keep it visible in the dish.

Pakistani Chicken Broast & French Fries

SNACK

Sabeen made this western dish her own by using local Pakistani spices. Her clients loved this light and delicious snack and served it with garlic sauce. It was a very regular feature in Sabeen's weekly tiffin.

INGREDIENTS

- 1 kg Chicken (Cut in 12 pieces)
- 1 tsp Salt
- 1 tsp Mustard powder
- 1 tsp Paprika Powder
- 4 tsp Milk
- 4 tsp Lemon Juice
- 1 tsp White Pepper
- 1 cup Flour
- 1 Egg
- 1-2 tbsp Sunflower Oil for frying

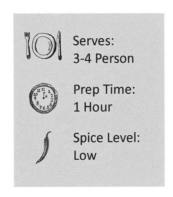

Serves:
3-4 Person

Prep Time:
1 Hour

Spice Level:
Low

METHOD

- Marinate chicken with lemon and salt. Leave it for half an hour.
- Mix all the dry ingredients. Also, mix egg and milk.
- Dip the chicken pieces in the batter and then in dry ingredients mixture. Leave it for 20 mins.
- Heat oil in a pan. Fry till golden brown on medium heat.
- Serve with French fries and ketchup.

Sabeen Secrets:

- Always make this dish in a deep fryer which helps pack the taste and keep the chicken moist. Follow the cooking time instructions as timing is everything in this dish.
- Cook French fries in the same oil since it acquires the flavour of the chicken.

Chicken Mayo Sandwiches

SNACK

There were two things I was sure of when I started dating Sabeen; she loves me and sandwiches! Chicken Mayo Sandwiches were her favourite snack when working in Aga Khan University Hospital. Later, she included them in her party menu, and they were very popular among her clients and at home. These are probably the best sandwiches that you will ever lay your hands on.

INGREDIENTS

- 2 cups Chicken (Boil and finely shredded)
- 3-4 tbsp Mayonnaise
- 1 tbsp Cream
- ½ tsp White Pepper
- Salt to taste
- Cucumber Crushed 1tbsp
- 4 slices White Bread

Serves:
4-5 Person

Prep Time:
40 minutes

Spice Level:
Low

METHOD

- In a bowl, add boiled chicken, mayonnaise and all the spices. Mix well.
- Now take bread slices and cut off the sides.
- Spread the mixture on one side of the slice and cover it with another.
- Cut them into four equal parts.
- Serve with fries.

Sabeen Secrets:

- You can also toast the bread as this will help retain its shape. However, for a softer experience, use the bread as is.
- Chicken should be shredded as fine as possible to avoid having big chunks in every bite.
- Use good quality mayo since the taste of mayo is key to the most delicious sandwiches.

Stir Fry Chicken & Vegetable Noodles

MAIN

Sabeen made these simple yet extremely delicious noodles when we wanted to eat Chinese. They are loaded with colourful vegetables and packed with the flavour of various sauces used during the cooking process. These noodles were a regular feature in food that Sabeen supplied for parties.

INGREDIENTS

- 300 gm Chicken (Cut in thin strips)
- 1 tbsp Dark Soy Sauce
- 1 tsp Brown Sugar
- 1 tbsp Vinegar
- 1 tbsp Corn Flour
- 1 tsp Salt
- 1 tsp Crushed Red Chilli
- 150 gms Bamboo Shoots
- 5-6 Garlic Cloves (Chopped)
- 3 Carrots (Thinly sliced)
- 1 Red and Green Capsicum (Thinly sliced)
- ½ cup Mushrooms (Thinly sliced)
- ¼ cup Chicken Broth
- ½ cup Spring Onions
- 300 gms Egg Noodles
- 4 tbsp Sunflower Oil
- 1 tbsp Sesame Oil
- 1½ tsp Black Pepper
- 2 tsp Fresh Lime Juice

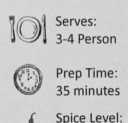

Serves:
3-4 Person

Prep Time:
35 minutes

Spice Level:
Low

METHOD

- Boil water and then remove from heat. Drop the egg noodles in this water and soak for 15-20 minutes to cook them. Stir occasionally to separate the noodles. Keep it aside.
- Take a bowl and mix dark soy sauce, vinegar, brown sugar, cornflour, and crushed red chilli.
- In a pan, add oil and fry chicken on high heat with salt and pepper for 7-8 minutes. Keep it aside.
- Take a wok and heat the oil, add chopped garlic and sauté for few minutes. Then add carrots, capsicum and mushroom and stir fry for 3-4 minutes on medium to high flame.
- Then add the mixture of soy sauce to it and mix well. Add chicken, lime juice, chicken broth and let it cook for 2-3 minutes.
- Now add vegetables, sesame oil and toss it well.
- Garnish it with spring onions and serve hot.

Sabeen Secrets:

- You can also increase the heat by adding more crushed chilli and chilli oil.
- This dish also goes well with Udon Noodles.

Cheesecake

DESSERT

This is baking heaven and every baker's dream to perfect. Our whole family loved cheesecakes, and we used to go to the Cheesecake Factory in Dubai Mall often to enjoy the variety and taste. Here is Sabeen's recipe, which is easy to make.

INGREDIENTS

Crust

- 2 cups Digestive Biscuits (About 16-18)
- 85 gms Butter (Melted)
- 1 tbsp Granulated Sugar
- ½ tsp Salt

Cheesecake Filling

- 950 gms Cream Cheese (Room temperature)
- 350 gms Granulated Sugar
- 3 tbsp Flour (Sieved)
- ½ cup Sour Cream (Room temperature)
- 2 tsp Vanilla Extract
- 3 Eggs (Room temperature)
- 1 tsp Lemon Juice

 Serves: 3-4 Person

 Prep Time: 1.5 hours

METHOD

Making the Crust:

- Put the biscuit crumbs salt and sugar in a mixer (food processor) and mix till it becomes fine crumbs. Then add melted butter while also pulsing.
- Put baking paper at the bottom of the cake pan and press the mixture into the bottom and up the sides.
- Preheat the oven at 180-degree Celsius and bake the crust for 8 minutes, or until lightly golden. Set aside while you make the cheesecake filling.

Making the Cheesecake:

- For the cream, in the bowl of an electric mixer fitted with the paddle attachment, mix the cream cheese and sugar (adding gradually) on medium speed until smooth (about 2-3 minutes), scraping the sides of the bowl as necessary. Add half tsp of salt halfway and keep mixing.
- Now keep the mixer on low speed and add the sour cream, lemon juice and vanilla extract. Mix well, scraping sides of the bowl as necessary.
- Now add flour and mix again. Keep scraping the bowl.
- Add the eggs (one at a time), mixing at low speed after each addition. Don't over mix here, as the batter should be smooth, light, glossy and somewhat airy.
- Pour the filling over the crust and spread evenly with a spatula.
- Now put in the oven for the first 10 minutes at 180-degree Celsius and then turn it down to 150-degree. Bake for 40 minutes.
- Carefully run a knife around the rim of the pan to loosen the cake. Allow the cheesecake to cool at room temperature for at least an hour, then cover and transfer into the refrigerator for 6 hours or overnight. Release the sides of the springform pan before slicing.
- Top it up with strawberries, blueberries, or even figs. All go with this cake.

Sabeen Secrets:

- With crumbs, remember that butter is used as a binding agent. So, once you make the mixture stick together in a spoon and it forms a shape of a ball, the base of the cheesecake is ready.
- To line up the crumbs mixture evenly and nicely in the baking tin, take a glass and press the bottom against the mixture slowly.
- While mixing cream cheese in a mixer, use a spatula to scrape the sides and bottom, so all ingredients are well mixed.

WHAT A PRANKSTER

In college, Sabeen was a very fun-loving young lady. This is where she really blossomed into both a serial prankster and an extremely loving and compassionate person. She was very popular in college and had many friends. People knew her due to her kind and fun-loving nature.

Although a brilliant student, she always sat at the back of the class in Commerce College with her friends. She played many pranks while enjoying college life. She used to make paper balls and throw them at students in the front. People really got irritated. Her friends tried to learn how to make them but weren't able to get the right size or shape.

She also used to make firecracker sounds from drinking straws, and when the teacher looked towards them, her innocent face never gave her away!

She used to play with one of her friend's hair, putting dried leaves and sticks in various knots when she was not looking. Later, her friend had to shake them all out, which took some time.

Along with her friends, Sabeen took common room cash from the new junior student batch and bought Ice Cream with it.

Her prankster trait carried into her early professional life. While working for Aga Khan University Hospital IT department in Karachi, all her colleagues loved her due to her fun nature. Her pranks helped to keep the working environment enjoyable. She was very happy with her job.

Her light nature kept her looking young and naughty throughout her adult life. As they say, you look outside what you feel inside, and that's exactly how Sabeen was. She didn't have a single white hair when she turned 40, while I had many!

The next chapter celebrates Sabeen's fun side. Here are some recipes that you can make with your family or friends that are sure to bring joy to your table.

Cheese Mini Pastries

SNACK

One of the most favourite creations of Sabeen. Crunchy yet soft, with the most delicious toppings and complimented with gooey cheese. Yum!

INGREDIENTS

- 500 gm Puff Pastry
- 30 gm Butter
- 1 tsp Salt
- 1 tsp Black Pepper
- 300 gm Portobello Mushrooms
- 1 Tomato (Cut in very small pieces)
- 1 Onion, Finely Chopped
- 100 gm Mozzarella Cheese
- 2 Eggs (Beaten)
- 1 Garlic (Chopped in very small pieces)
- 1 cup Chopped Herbs (Parsley and Basil)

Serves:
2-3 Person

Prep Time:
45 minutes

METHOD

- Put butter in a pan and heat till it melts. Then add mushrooms and fry for 3-4 minutes.
- Then add tomatoes, onions along with salt and pepper. Keep frying till tomatoes and onions become soft.
- Then add chopped herbs and fry for another 1-2 minutes. Now put aside.
- Lay flat the puff pastry sheet and cut it into small equal rectangles.
- Brush these with egg wash and then top each with the mushroom mixture we cooked.
- Add mozzarella cheese on top and put in the oven at 200-degree Celsius for 20-25 minutes.

Pakoras

SNACK

Pakoras are a delicious Pakistani fried snack. They are crisp on the outside and soft on the inside, usually enjoyed with Sabeen's Pakora chutney. This is a very common dish to eat during the rainy season in Pakistan or during Ramadan when people break their fast. You can make many variations of Pakoras: vegetable, potatoes, chicken, aubergines, spinach leaves, etc. Once the batter is ready, then anything can be dipped and fried – use your imagination!

INGREDIENTS

- 1 cup Gram Flour
- 6 Onions (Medium sliced)
- 1 tsp Red Chili
- ½ tsp Chat Masala
- 1 tsp Salt
- ½ tsp Turmeric Powder
- 1 cup Coriander (Roughly chopped)

Serves:
2-3 Person

Prep Time:
30 minutes

Spice Level:
Low

METHOD

- Mix all the ingredients with water to make a smooth paste.
- Heat the oil in a skillet. The flame should be high till the oil gets hot, and then make it medium before frying.
- Use your hand and start putting the mixture in the skillet. Fry till the pakoras turn golden brown.
- Line a plate with a paper towel. Place all the pakoras on the plate to absorb excess oil. Sprinkle chat masala on top.
- Serve it with Sabeen's Pakora chutney.

SABEEN'S PAKORA CHUTNEY

- 2 Onions
- 5-6 Green Chillies
- 1 tsp Cumin Seeds
- 1 Bulb of Garlic (Chopped)
- 2 tbsp Oil
- 1 tbsp Tamarind (Remove the seeds)

First, fry the onions. Once they are soft, add green chillies, cumin seeds and garlic. Fry for 2-3 minutes. Then grind this mixture (remove excess oil) along with tamarind. Once done, add 1 tbsp of excess oil.

Sabeen Secrets:

- It is important to get the batter right. Don't make it too runny or too pasty (hard).
- Don't overcook the Pakoras; only fry 4-5 minutes before taking it out.

DRUMS OF HEAVEN

SNACK

This really shows the fun side of Sabeen. Chicken winglets tossed in sweet and spicy sauce create such a unique taste profile. It's absolutely fabulous and enjoyable!

Serves:
4-5 Person

Prep Time:
40 minutes

INGREDIENTS

- 1 kg Chicken Winglets (Prepared as a lollipop)
- ½ tsp Cracked Black Pepper
- 1 tsp Kashmiri Chilli
- 1 tsp Salt
- 1½ tsp Ginger Garlic Paste
- 1 tbsp Dark Soya Sauce
- 1 tsp White Vinegar
- Sunflower Oil for Deep Frying

METHOD

Mix all the above together and marinate for 1 hour in the fridge. Then add 1tsp of cornflour, 3 tbsp of all-purpose flour. 1½ tsp of Kashmiri chilli, 1 egg, and mix together. Deep fry in hot oil for 5-10 minute till winglets are done.

SAUCE

- 1 tbsp Ginger (Chopped very small)
- 1 tbsp Garlic (Chopped very small)
- 1 Onion (Chopped in small pieces)
- 3 tbsp Schezwan Sauce
- 1 tsp Dark Soya Sauce
- 2 tbsp Tomato Ketchup
- 1 tsp Sugar
- 1 tsp White Vinegar
- 1 tsp Corn Flour Slurry

METHOD

Heat oil and then add ginger and garlic. Stir for 1-2 minutes and then add onions to sauté till it becomes translucent. Then add Schezwan Sauce and give it a good mix for 30 seconds. Then add soya sauce and tomato ketchup while stirring. Add sugar, white vinegar and stir. Finally, add corn slurry and keep stirring till the sauce becomes thick.

SERVINGS

Now add the chicken winglets and mix well till sauce binds to the winglets. Then add 2 tbsp chopped spring onion (green parts) and mix again. Drums of Heaven are ready!

Vanilla Bean Chocolate Cupcakes

DESSERT

If you want to know what heaven feels like, eat these cupcakes! They are a beautiful combination of chocolate and vanilla topped with vanilla bean buttercream frosting. Sabeen was an expert cupcake maker and also made these for several charity events.

 Serves: 3-4 Person

 Prep Time: 40 minutes

INGREDIENTS

Chocolate Cupcakes

- 2 Eggs
- 1 cup Extra Fine Sugar
- ¼ cup Vegetable Oil
- ½ cup Milk
- 1 tsp Vanilla Extract
- 1 cup All-Purpose Flour
- ½ cup Unsweetened Cocoa Powder
- ½ tsp Baking Powder
- Pinch of Salt

Vanilla Bean Buttercream

- 1 cup Butter (Room temperature)
- 1 Vanilla Bean
- 3 cups Powdered Sugar
- 1-2 tbsp Heavy Cream (Optional)

METHOD

- Heat the oven to 200-degree Celsius.
- Line 10 cupcake cups with paper baking cups. Set aside.
- In a mixing bowl, add the eggs, sugar and vegetable oil.
- With the paddle attachment on, beat on medium-high speed for 1 to 2 minutes or until well mixed.
- In a small bowl, combine the flour, cocoa powder, baking powder, and salt.
- Alternately, add the flour mixture with the milk and beat until blended.
- Divide the batter evenly among the prepared cupcake cups.
- Bake in preheated oven for 18 minutes or until a toothpick inserted in the centre comes out clean.
- Remove from the oven and cool completely on a wire rack.
- In a mixing bowl, add the butter. With the paddle attachment on, beat on low speed until light and fluffy, for about 3-5minutes.
- Meanwhile, split the vanilla bean lengthwise into two halves with a sharp paring knife, holding onto the bean's "hook" with your fingers.
- With the flat, unsharpened side of the knife, scrape the seeds as much as possible from the two vanilla bean halves.
- Add the vanilla seeds to the creamed butter.
- Gently beat in the powder sugar, a little at a time.
- When all the sugar is added, increase the mixer's speed to medium-high and beat for 2-3 more minutes.
- If you think your frosting is too thick, add a few drops of heavy cream until you reach desired consistency.
- Spoon the frosting into a piping bag fitted with a frosting tip and frost the cooled cupcakes.

<

 pinkoveninfo   ...

View Insights   Promote

 Liked by **madiha.siddiqui.5** and **24 others**

pinkoveninfo Pink Oven's Vanilla Bean and Chocolate
Fudge Cupcakes for Alzheimer Research Center
Charity Event in Orleans Park School #cupcakes
#alzheimersawareness #charityevent #chocolate
#vanilla #cupcaketower #london #londonevents
#richmonduk #orleansparkschool

Gol Gappa

SNACK

What a fun snack this is from the streets of Karachi. It's very crispy, bite-size fried balls, which are hollow in the middle for the filling. Sabeen loved having these while growing up in Karachi. This is a perfect tribute to her fun-filled, sweet and sour nature.

INGREDIENTS

- 1 Box of Ready-Made Gol Gappa Balls (Easier than making yourself)
- 250 gms Boiled Chickpeas
- 100 gms boiled potatoes (Cut in nine squares)
- 3-4 Tomatoes (Cut in very small pieces)
- 2 Onions (Cut in very small pieces)

Green Chutney (Sour) Prep:
- 1 Mint Bundle
- 1 Coriander Bundle
- 1 tbsp Cumin Seeds
- 3 Green Chillies (Whole)
- 5 Cloves of Garlic (Whole)
- 1 tsp Salt
- 2 tbsp Lemon Juice
- 2 cups Water

Put all ingredients in the blender and blend.

Serves:
4-5 Person

Prep Time:
40 minutes

Brown Chutney (Sweet) Prep:
- 100 gm Imli/Tamarind Water (Soak in warm water for 20 minutes and then hand squeezed through a sieve in a bowl under. Continue to squeeze the seeds so that all juices from the pulp pass through the sieve and get collected in the bowl below. At the end you should have 1 kg tamarind water)
- 200 gm Gur/Jaggery
- 2 tbsp Condensed Milk
- 1 tsp Garam Masala
- 1 tsp Black Salt
- 1 tsp Salt
- 1 tsp Red Chilli Powder

Mix all of the above and cook on high heat till it boils and then lower heat to keep cooking till it thickens. Keep stirring occasionally.

SERVING

Now take each Gol Gappa and fill with chickpeas, potatoes, and pour sweet and sour chutneys on top. Then just pop in your mouth and enjoy!

Butter Chicken

MAIN

This is one of Sabeen's favourite dishes, and she would always suggest making it when we didn't know what to have that day. She had her own take on it, which we are sharing with you to prepare a tender, flavour infused chicken with rich butter gravy. One look at it, and you want to dive right in!

Serves: 3-4 Person

Prep Time: 1 Hour

Spice Level: Low

INGREDIENTS

Marinate:
- 500 gm Chicken (Boneless cut in medium pieces)
- 1 tsp Red Chilli
- 1 tsp Ginger Garlic Paste
- 2 tsp Yoghurt
- 1 tsp Kashmiri Red Chilli Powder
- ½ tsp Garam Masala Powder
- ½ tsp Salt

Gravy:
- 2 Onions (Chopped small)
- 3 Large Tomatoes (Chopped)
- 1 tsp Ginger Garlic Paste
- ½ cup Double Cream
- 2 tsp Kashmiri Chilli Powder
- ½ tsp Garam Masala
- ½ tsp Turmeric
- 1 tsp Cumin Powder
- 1 tsp Coriander Powder
- 1 tsp Dry Fenugreek
- 10 Cashew Nuts
- Chopped Coriander leaves (Few strands)
- 1 tsp Salt
- 2 tbsp Oil
- 200 gm Butter

METHOD

- Marinate the chicken with all ingredients and leave for 1 hour in the fridge.
- Now add 1 tbsp oil in a pan and fry the marinated chicken for 10 minutes and keep aside.
- Now add 100 gm butter and 1 tbsp oil in a large pot. Once hot, add onions to saute till soft.
- Add ginger-garlic paste and fry. Now add tomatoes.
- Now add all spices (add only half Kashmiri red chilli powder) and bhono by adding little water in intervals.
- Now add half a cup of water till tomatoes are cooked through (they are mushy). Then add cashew nuts and fry for 5 minutes.
- Cool the masala and now add in a blender with ½ cup of water to blend.
- In the same pan, add 100 grams of butter and add remaining Kashmiri red chilli powder to fry at low flame for 5 minutes.
- Now add the blended masala paste and fry for 5-7 minutes. If the blended masala is very thick, just add a little warm water.
- Add the fried chicken to this paste and mix well. Then add cream and let it simmer for 10 minutes on low heat.
- Add chopped coriander, fenugreek and mix well.
- Add fresh cream on top in a circle pattern to serve.

Sabeen Secrets:

- Sabeen would actually add a blob of butter on top as well to give it an inviting look.

Chicken Lasagne

MAIN

This is the hallmark of Italian cooking and the ultimate comfort food. The soft, gooey taste of Sabeen's Lasagne combined with the bursting flavours of meat, cheese, and sauces, really makes it incredibly delicious. You need to give it a go.

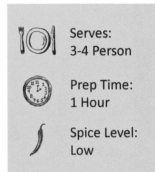

Serves:
3-4 Person

Prep Time:
1 Hour

Spice Level:
Low

INGREDIENTS

- ½ kg Chicken Mince
- 1 Onion (Finely chopped)
- 2 Garlic Cloves (Finely chopped)
- 200 ml Chicken Stock (1 Cube)
- ½ tsp Dried Oregano
- 1 tsp Red Chilli Powder
- 1 tsp Red Chilli Flakes
- ½ tsp Salt
- 1 tsp Cracked Black Pepper

- 500 gm Tomato Sauce
- 1 kg White Lasagne Sauce
- 6 Lasagne Sheets
- 1 kg Shredded Cheese (Mozzarella and Cheddar)
- 100 gm Parsley (¼ bundle, finely chopped)
- 2-3 Basil Leaves for Garnish
- 1 tbsp Olive Oil

METHOD

- Heat oil and fry the onions till the colour turns transparent. Then add garlic and fry till golden brown.
- Add chicken mince and fry for 10 minutes till it changes colour.
- Now add red chilli, red chilli powder, salt, cracked black pepper, oregano and fry for 3-4 minutes.
- Add tomato sauce and mix well. Then add chicken stock, one cup of water and cover the lid to cook for 15-20 minutes on low flame.
- Now take a glass baking dish or aluminium tray, grease with oil.
- Now for layering; first put the lasagne sheets, followed by cooked mince layer, first layer of cheese, second layer of lasgane sheets, second layer of cooked mince, white sauce, second layer of cheese, third layer of lasagne sheets and now put the final layer of cheese on top generously.
- Preheat oven to 180-degree Celsius and place the dish inside for 30-35 minutes. Cover the tray after the first 10 minutes with an aluminium foil so the cheese on top does not burn or become too dark in colour.
- Sprinkle parsley and put a couple of basil leaves on top to present the dish.

Sabeen Secrets:

- Only use pre-cooked Lasagne sheets, so you don't have to boil them.
- Check whether Lasagne is cooked by putting a wooden skewer through the layers. It should be soft as it is going in.

Creamy Mushroom Pasta

MAIN

This is one of the tastiest dishes from Sabeen. Garlic mushrooms mixed with creamy sauce and beautifully cooked pasta, which eventually gets folded together in the pan.

INGREDIENTS

- 500 gm Portobello Mushroom (Finely chopped)
- 2 Garlic Cloves (Finely chopped)
- 300 ml Double Cream
- 1 tsp Salt
- 1 tsp Cracked Black Pepper
- 1 Onion (Finely chopped)
- 150 gm Butter
- 300 gm Penne Pasta (Boiled and strained)
- 1 cup Grated Parmesan Cheese
- ½ cup Chopped Parsley
- 2 tbsp Olive Oil

Serves:
3-4 Person

Prep Time:
40-45 minutes

Spice Level:
Low

METHOD

- Fry the onions in oil till it becomes transparent (15 minutes) on medium heat, and then add black pepper and salt. Fry for another 2 minutes. Turn off the heat.
- Now fry butter in oil for 3 minutes and then add mushrooms. Fry for 3-4 minutes, and then add some water to cook for another 5 minutes.
- Now add the caramelised onion and chopped garlic, fry for 2 minutes and then add the double cream. Mix well and cook for 3-4 minutes.
- Add the cooked pasta and mix well till sauce has completely covered the pasta.
- Take out the pasta in a dish and add parmesan cheese on top.
- Sprinkle chopped parsley for garnishing.

Sabeen Secrets:

- Make sure that pasta is not overcooked as it will become hard and chewy.

BAKING DIARIES

Sabeen always had an interest in baking and used to make cakes, cookies, and brownies at home during her college and university days. In fact, people visiting her parents' house would keenly enquire if any of her cakes were available to eat. This is where Sabeen picked up her kitchen skills and discipline. This was also her initial motivation to start Pink Oven, focusing on cupcakes, cakes, cookies, and brownies.

Yummy Brownies

This passion continued into our marriage, and I developed a sweet tooth during our life together, although I wasn't very keen on it earlier.

Some of her early baking efforts.

Sabeen always made special efforts for our Son's birthday.

Delicious Cookies, which my younger sister loved!

....and she also loved sharing them on social media.

While we were living in Singapore, Sabeen started taking professional cupcake baking and decorating classes.

Also, some very crafty and nice cakes.

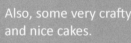

The next chapter takes you on a whirlwind tour of some of Sabeen's sweet and yummy classics from her early baking days:

Vanilla Sponge Cake

DESSERT

This is from Sabeen's college days when she was baking at home. Sabeen's cakes were always soft and delicious, and this very special recipe should be done with a lot of love and care. The cake turns out very well if you use the correct measurements. Some of Sabeen's clients refused to have their party cakes done anywhere else but from her.

INGREDIENTS

- 226 gm Unsalted Butter (Softened)
- 300 gm Granulated or Caster Sugar
- 4 Eggs (Room temperature)
- 1 tbsp Vanilla Extract
- 330 gm Self-Raising Cake Flour
- 2¾ tsp Baking Powder
- ½ tsp Salt
- 240 ml Whole Milk (Room temperature)

Serves:
5-6 Person

Prep Time:
1.5 hours

METHOD

- In a large bowl, beat the butter and sugar together using an electric mixer until light and fluffy (about 5 minutes).
- Add the eggs, one at a time, mixing well after each addition. Beat in the vanilla.
- Combine the flour (pass through a sieve), baking powder, and salt in a medium bowl.
- Stir with a whisk and add it to the butter mixture, followed by the milk. Beat on medium-low speed just until combined. We need to ensure that the mixture has a nice and smooth consistency.
- Preheat the oven to 180-degree Celsius.
- Line the bottom with parchment paper (cut to fit) and generously grease the parchment paper as well.
- Dust the pans with flour, then tap out any excess.
- Lightly grease the sides and bottom of 9-inch round cake pans with butter.
- Pour the batter into the prepared pan.
- Bake for 30-40 minutes or until a toothpick inserted into the centre comes out with few moist crumbs attached.

21:46

PINKOVENINFO
Posts

pinkoveninfo

If you are looking for a thoroughly professional service, who not only makes food with authentic flavour, but also adds in her personal touch and incorporates her clients needs wholeheartedly , then look no further.. use pink oven and I can assure you that you will not be disappointed...
From, A very satisfied customer

View Insights   Promote

Liked by old_isleworth_market and 22 others

pinkoveninfo Another review....#cake #cakelicious #buttercreamcake #greatbritain #food #hounslow #london #londonfood #pakistanicuisine #yummy #foodporn #foodphotography

Sabeen Secrets:

- Always keep all ingredients at room temperature.
- Always use a pan with removable bottom.
- If you want to make a coloured cake, you can add it once the batter is ready and mix it with a spatula.
- If you want to apply buttercream on top, then cut the cake in half with a very sharp knife. Apply buttercreams between the two parts and also then on the top and outer edges of the cake. Best to place the cake on a cake turntable for easy handling.
- Don't open the oven frequently to check the cake as this will disturb the temperature inside.

Chocolate Chip Cookies

DESSERT

This is the hallmark of Sabeen's baking delights. She started making these cookies at home and then offered them to her clients who just loved these. These were firm on the outside and soft and gooey from the inside. She was an amazing baker.

INGREDIENTS

- 380 gms All-Purpose Flour
- 1 tsp Baking Soda
- 1 tsp Salt
- 227 gms Unsalted Butter (Room temperature)
- 100 gms Granulated Sugar
- 1¼ cups Brown Sugar
- 2 tsp Vanilla Extract
- 2 Large Eggs (Room temperature)
- 2 cups Chocolate Chips

 Serves:
1-2 Person

 Prep Time:
40 minutes
(After 24 hours)

METHOD

- Preheat oven to 180-degree Celsius. Line baking sheet with parchment paper.
- In a medium bowl, combine the flour, baking soda, and salt.
- In the bowl of an electric mixer, beat the butter, granulated sugar and brown sugar until creamy, about 2 minutes. Add the vanilla and eggs. Gradually beat in the flour mixture. Stir in the chocolate chips.
- Wrap dough in plastic wrap and refrigerate for at least 24 hours. This allows the dough to "marinate" and makes the cookies thicker, chewier, and more flavourful.
- After this, let the dough sit at room temperature just until it is soft enough to scoop.
- Divide the dough into 4-tablespoon sized balls using a large cookie scoop and drop onto prepared baking sheets.
- Bake for 12-15 minutes, or until golden brown. Cool for 5 minutes before removing to wire racks to cool completely.

OUR LOVE STORY

I always felt that it was fate that brought us together in Karachi. I moved to Riyadh, Saudi Arabia, in 1986 and grew up there with my parents and three siblings. Although it was very boring to live in Saudi Arabia in those times (now it has transformed a lot and some things that are allowed today were unimaginable before), I also never wanted to go back to Pakistan. In fact, I wanted to go to the US for my higher education and even passed my International English Language Test (TOEFL) with flying colours. However, my father had strong ideas and decided to send me to Pakistan.

Once back in Pakistan, I was terribly upset and angry about his decision but did not have any choice. I tried to get admission into an Engineering University and, despite good grades, did not succeed since I was considered an international student and had to apply via a quota system. I then tried to get into a prestigious business school in Pakistan but could not pass the interview stage. I finally searched and discovered IoBM (Institute of Business Management, also known as CBM) in 1997, a relatively unknown business school at that time.

My uncle, who was helping me with the admissions process, was quite surprised by my selection, particularly because it was very far away from where I lived. I didn't even have a car, so I had to travel by public bus, which is not very pleasant in Pakistan.

Sabeen was already enrolled in IoBM and was part of one of the first few student cohorts that joined the college. She was very attractive, popular and also had many friends that admired her. Many boys were very keen on being friends with her. Along with having fun, she remained a brilliant student, and all teachers respected her.

I first met Sabeen in our college van, since coincidently our houses were near to each other. The same van picked us up, and we started chatting together. It was all fun and games while travelling to and back from college.

I started visiting her house to give her support in certain subjects, which I was good at and where I could help her. I used to get along well with her family, and they insisted that I come more often. I started getting involved in their daily life and used to go out with them for breakfasts and dinners. Since I was living alone with my elder sister, they gave me a sense of family. I liked Sabeen a lot, but there were no intimate feelings between us in the beginning; we just enjoyed each other's company even though we came from very different backgrounds. This is one of her beautiful traits that I will speak more about later.

I was also very protective of her, and if she ever got in trouble, I would be the first one to get involved and help her. She had many male friends, but she valued my company and the trouble I went to take care of her. Maybe this was the start of our love without even realising it. Once a lecturer told us that the amount of trouble you take for someone shows the love you have for them. I strongly believe in this.

Slowly, we started to come closer and developed feelings for each other. I was the first one to say "I love you" to her, and she, being shy, took some time to return the three magic words that would change the world for us. We started spending more time together, held hands in the van and eventually became a couple. However, it was not an easy progression into our relationship.

Sabeen's parents were not very keen on our relationship initially. I came from a humble background and was still studying, while Sabeen was well taken care of in every respect. I was told that I should focus on my studies and start my career rather than getting into a relationship with Sabeen. Traditionally, Pakistani girls are married by the age of 21-22, and it would have taken me longer than this to stand on my own feet and give her a good life. It was a tense period for both of us since we wanted nothing else other than being together.

This revelation resulted in my restricted contact with Sabeen; her parents naturally put restrictions on our meetups (that's very normal behaviour in Pakistan, where parents are not very happy with a relationship, although quite uncalled for). We used to meet up in college or sometimes in malls, etc. My friends helped me a lot during this time. We were hurting, and I eventually had to seek the help of my parents to convince Sabeen's parents about the seriousness of our relationship. The most difficult person to convince was Sabeen's mother, who is very stubborn (even to this day) and always wanted her to get married into a rich family so she can

continue enjoying the lifestyle they always gave her. I didn't blame her since all parents want the best for their child.

However, our resolve was stronger than their stubbornness, and eventually, Sabeen's father relented since he loved her a lot. We were engaged and destined to be married together when I was ready financially.

I started working for Citibank while doing my Bachelor of Business Administration (BBA) and Master of Business Administration (MBA) to stand on my feet as soon as possible. We did our MBA together and achieved very good grades, and instantly got jobs at better places. This helped steady the ship as we neither compromised our studies nor lost focus on what we wanted to achieve. I give a lot of credit to Sabeen since she was in a more hostile environment than me, but she never gave up. She loved me so very much. It felt destiny for us to be together. Forever.

I eventually got a job at a global Marketing Research company called Ipsos in Dubai and decided to move since it would mean a better life for Sabeen (which always remained very important for me) and would also give us financial stability.

The next chapter contains some recipes that we loved having together during our courtship.

SHAMI KEBAB

SNACK

Shami kebab literally means "Syrian Kebabs". It is one of the most loved kebabs in Pakistan and was certainly for Sabeen as well. We used to have it at breakfast with Paratha and Egg or with Daal at lunch or dinner. It was also a favourite among Pink Oven's clients and was often served at our market stalls.

Serves:
5-6 Person

Prep Time:
1 hour

Spice Level:
Medium

INGREDIENTS

- 1 kg Boneless Lamb (Cut into medium pieces)
- 2 tbsp Whole Coriander Seeds
- 1 tsp Cumin Seeds
- 1 tsp Salt
- 1 Onion (Chopped roughly in medium pieces)
- ½ tsp Garam Masala
- 10 Whole Red Chilli
- ½ kg Chana Daal (Boiled and fully cooked)
- 1½ tsp Ginger Garlic Paste

- 1 tsp Garam Masala Powder
- 2 Eggs
- 4 Green Chilies (Finely chopped)
- 3-4 Mint Strands
- 1 Fresh Coriander Bundle (Finely chopped)
- 1 tsp Lemon Juice
- 1 tbsp Sunflower Oil

METHOD

- Put meat, coriander seeds, onion, ginger garlic paste, cumin seeds, salt, red chilli and little oil in 2-3 glasses of water to boil on medium heat.
- Once the meat is fully cooked, remove it from the heat and make sure that some water in the pot is retained.
- Put this mixture along with very little water from the mixture and boiled chana daal in a chopper and grind thoroughly till all ingredients are mixed well. The texture here should not be runny, rather thickish but not dry.
- Once done, add eggs, coriander, green chillies, mint and a little lemon juice. Mix well with your hands.
- Leave to rest for 1 hour in the fridge.
- Make round shaped kebabs with your hands and fry in oil till light brown on both sides. This should not take 5 minutes on each side as the meat is already done.

Sabeen Secrets:

- Don't put too much juice from the boiled meat in the grinder, as this will make the mixture runny. A little bit of juice is added to make the mixture moist.
- You can also freeze the shaped kebabs (before frying) and use them for one month.

Special Chana Chat

SNACK

This snack is one of my favourites. It combines the softness of chickpeas, the bursting flavours of spices and the crunchiness of Chat Papri (deep-fried, crisp, small flour crackers). It is served topped with sweet and savoury chutneys. Is your mouth drooling already?

 Serves:
3-4 Person

 Prep Time:
25 minutes

 Spice Level:
Low

INGREDIENTS

- 2 cups Chickpeas
- 2 tbsp Tamarind Sauce
- 2 tsp Chat Masala
- 1 cup Sabeen's Green Sauce
- 1 tsp Salt
- 1 Onion (Medium chopped)
- 1 Tomato (Medium chopped)
- 1 tsp Baking Soda
- Papri

Sabeen's Green Sauce:

- 1 Coriander Bundle (Roughly chopped)
- 3-4 Mint Strands (Roughly chopped)
- 1 cup Yoghurt
- 1 tsp Sugar
- ½ tsp Salt
- ½ tsp Pepper
- Blend together all the above ingredients

METHOD

- Soak the chickpeas overnight with baking soda.
- The next day, rinse the chickpeas and boil them with water and salt till soft.
- Take a bowl and put chickpeas, both the sauces, chat masala, onions and tomatoes. Mix it well.
- Garnish with Papri.

Dahi Bara (Lentil Dumplings in Sweetened Yoghurt)

SNACK

If Chana Chat (see page 62) is the king of Pakistani snacks, this is the Queen. Sabeen's Dahi Baras were so beautifully presented that one look of the finished dish made you want to dive in. The dish is finished perfectly with a sprinkle of some chat masala or Dahi Bara masala on top.

INGREDIENTS

- 500 gm White Lentil
- 1 tsp Roasted Cumin
- 1 tsp Roasted Coriander
- 5-7 Whole Red Chillies
- ¼ tsp Baking Soda
- 1 tsp Salt
- 3-4 cups Oil for Deep Frying
- 4 cups Yogurt (Baras should be submerged)
- Water to Soak Baras
- 2-3 tbsp Icing Sugar
- Red Chilli Powder

Serves:
4 Person

Prep Time:
30-35 minutes

Spice Level:
Low

METHOD

- Wash and soak white lentil overnight.
- Coarsely crush roasted cumin, coriander, and whole red chillies.
- Put soaked White lentil in a blender, add half of the roasted cumin, coriander, and red chilli powder and keep half aside.
- Add baking soda and salt. Now blend all the ingredients well add water as required. The mixture should not be runny.
- Make medium size baras and deep fry them.
- Beat the yoghurt, add a little salt in it, then add baras and cover them with yoghurt. Sprinkle the left-over powder on it to garnish.

Liver Masala (Beef or Lamb)

MAIN

This dish simply has yay or nay sayers... no-one in-between! You either like Liver, or you don't, but the people who like it will enjoy this Sabeen special a lot. I used to request her to make this for my breakfast on Big Eid (Eid Al-Adha, where Muslims sacrifice animals and Hajj also takes place) when we got the meat of our sacrificial animal. She always made funny faces, but eventually cooked it for me as she loved me a lot! Enjoy it with Naan.

INGREDIENTS

- 1 Full Liver Piece (Cleaned, washed and cut into small pieces)
- 2½ tsp Ginger Garlic Paste
- 1 tsp Salt
- 1 tsp Fennel Seeds
- 1 tsp Dry Fenugreek
- 1 tsp Kalonji
- 1 Medium Size Onion (Grinded)
- 2 Tomatoes (Chopped)
- 1 cup Yoghurt (Whisked)
- 1 tsp Red Chilli

- 1½ tsp Coarsely Ground Coriander Seed
- 1 tsp Cumin Powder
- ½ tsp Turmeric Powder (Haldi)
- ¼ tsp Garam Masala
- Chopped coriander
- Finely Chopped Ginger
- 4 Green Chilies (2 whole and 2 chopped)
- 1 tbsp Sunflower Oil
- 2 tsp Ghee

 Serves: 2-3 Person

 Prep Time: 1 Hour

 Spice Level: Medium

METHOD

- Heat ghee and oil in a pot. Add ginger garlic paste and Bhono.
- Then add liver pieces and bhono with soft hands, high heat for 5 minutes and then lower the heat to cook the liver.
- In another wok, add 1 tsp ghee, kalonji, fennel seeds, fenugreek and onion. Bhono well.
- Then add all spices and then bhono again.
- Then add tomatoes and cook well. Once cooked, add yoghurt at low heat. Bhono.
- Now add liver into this gravy and mix well.
- Finally, add garam masala, green chillies (chopped and whole), as well as finely chopped ginger. Once Masala has completely dried, Liver Masala is done.

Galawati Chops

Serves: 4-5 Person Prep Time: 1.5 Hours Spice Level: Medium

SABEEN SIGNATURE/MAIN

Galawati Chops are not very commonly made in Pakistan but are unique in taste and flavour. It is a marination base dish but cooked in a traditional way. Sabeen made it with a lot of skill and love.

INGREDIENTS

- 1 kg Lamb Chops
- 2 Onions (Finely chopped)
- Amchur (Dried mango powder)
- 6 Cloves
- 3 Bay Leaves
- 1 tsp Cumin Seeds
- 2 Tomatoes (Medium chopped)
- 1½ tsp Ginger Garlic Paste
- 4 Green Chilies (Whole)
- 1 tbsp Dried Papaya Powder or Meat Tenderiser (Mixed in water)
- 1 tsp Salt
- 1 tsp Cracked Black Pepper

- 1 Coriander Bundle (Chopped)
- 1 tbsp Ginger (Finely chopped)
- ½ tsp Garam Masala Powder
- ½ tsp Red Chilli
- 1 tbsp Ginger (Thinly sliced)
- 3-4 tbsp Sunflower Oil
- 1 tsp Ghee

METHOD

- Mix salt, cumin seeds, garam masala, black pepper, mango powder, ginger garlic paste, and yoghurt
- Add chops to this mixture and marinate. Leave for 30 minutes.
- Heat oil and ghee in a pot at medium heat. Add bay leaves, cumin seeds and cloves. Fry for 2-3 minutes.
- Now add onions and fry till golden brown.
- Add marinated chops and mix well. Then add tomatoes and green chillies and mix again.
- Now cover the pot and let it cook at low heat till chops are cooked through.
- Then add garam masala and red chilli powder, and bhono well.
- Add chopped coriander and ginger slices on top to present a colourful dish.

Sabeen Secrets:

- Marinating the chops will infuse the flavours within the meat, so always keep it aside for at least 30 minutes and better overnight.
- If you feel the gravy is less, add some water and cook on low heat till it thickens.

Tandoori Wings

SNACK

This is one of Sabeen's succulent dishes. This was her creative take on desi wings which is first fried in a pan and then put in an oven to lock in the flavours. Marination also makes the meat super tender, and the tandoori masala gives the wings that great colour.

Serves:
4-5 Person

Prep Time:
1 Hour

Spice Level:
Medium

INGREDIENTS

1 kg Chicken wings (Washed and drained)
1 tbsp Tandoori Masala:

- 2 tsp Coriander Powder
- 1½ tbsp Cumin Powder
- 1 tsp Garlic Powder
- 1 tsp Ginger Powder
- 1 tsp (6-8) Cloves
- 1 tsp Mace Powder
- 1 tsp Fenugreek
- 1 tsp Cinnamon Powder
- ½ tsp Nutmeg Powder

Grind all of the below together to make Tandoori Masala.

- ½ tsp Chat Masala
- 1 tbsp Yoghurt
- ½ tsp Salt
- ½ tsp Black Pepper Powder
- ½ tsp Chilli Sauce
- ½ tbsp Lemon Juice
- 1 tsp Red Food Colour

METHOD

- Marinate wings with all the ingredients and leave for 30 minutes.
- To cook the wings, you can bake or fry them.
- Heat oil in a pan, add your wings and shallow fry 10-15 mins each side.
- Then put it in the oven for 20 minutes.
- Once cooked, garnish with fresh coriander.

Sabeen Secrets:

- Serve with Sabeen's Green Sauce, don't eat with ketchup!

Pakistani Style Trifle

Serves: Prep Time:
3-4 Person   35-40 Minutes

SABEEN SIGNATURE/DESSERT

This is one of the most popular comfort desserts in Pakistan. This is also Sabeen's signature dessert and a heaven for people with a sweet tooth. It has multiple layers of delight that woos your palate and delight your senses. It is made on various occasions in Pakistan.

INGREDIENTS

- 2 cups of Milk
- 3 tbsp Sugar
- 1 Pack Strawberry Jelly
- 1 Tin of Fruit Cocktail (With syrup)
- 1-2 Bananas (Thinly sliced)
- Whipped Cream
- Vanilla Bean Pods (Add in whipped cream)
- 3-4 Cherries
- 450 gm Vanilla Sponge Cake
- Chocolate Cake Crumbs for garnish

Custard Mixture Preparation

- 500 ml Full Cream Milk
- ½ tsp of Cardamom
- 5 tbsp Granulated Sugar
- 2 tbsp Custard Powder (Heaped)
- 1 Drop of Vanilla Essence (or Extract)
- 3-4 tbsp Evaporated Milk

METHOD

- Start with preparing the custard. Mix custard powder with 2-3 tbsp of milk in a bowl and keep aside. It should be a liquid texture.
- Boil milk and evaporated milk along with sugar in a pot on medium flame. Bring to almost boiling point before taking it to lower the flame.
- Add cardamom, vanilla essence and then custard mixture. Keep stirring until it thickens.
- Once it thickens, move it off the flame. Make sure there are no lumps.
- Pour in a bowl and leave to set in a fridge.
- Now mix jelly mixture in hot water. Then add cold water to mix. Then once it cools down, put it in the fridge to set.
- For whipping cream, put a deep bowl in the freezer so it becomes super cold. Now put heavy whipping cream, 1 tbsp of sugar and one strand of Vanilla Bean Pod. Whisk with a whisker for about 3 minutes till it becomes firm with soft peaks. You can also use an electric mixer.
- Now take a deep serving bowl. Cut the cake into squares and put it in the bottom of the bowl to form the first layer.
- Now drizzle the juice of the fruit cocktail onto the cake and then pour in the first layer of custard.
- Now add the strawberry jelly layer followed by the second layer of custard.
- Then add a fruit cocktail and sliced bananas.
- Then add the final layer of custard. Add whipped cream on top and spread it evenly. Then put in 2-3 blobs of jelly in the middle.
- Now make the crumbs of vanilla and chocolate cake. Line them around the edges of the bowl as a garnish.
- Put in the cherry in the middle as well, and then you are done!

PAKISTANI TRIFLE

MARRIAGE, PARENTHOOD AND TRAVEL

We eventually got married on July 2, 2004, which was the happiest day of our lives. In Pakistani culture, the marriage ceremony lasts more than one day – ours spanned four full days of rituals, including two Mehndi's, a Rukhsati (the bride leaving parents' house to live with the husband), and Valima (the groom's dinner party). It was a fun event for everyone in our family & friends who felt relieved to celebrate the union of two people in love. I felt like the luckiest person on Earth that day as I was given the most beautiful and precious gift that would never be better than anything else.

In Pakistan, usually, brides are very emotional on their wedding day, as they are leaving their family home for the first time. However, Sabeen was so happy with our union that she didn't even cry. She was sad, of course, for leaving her parents but happier in finally being with me.
My family arranged our wedding room very nicely with candles and lots of flowers; however, being clumsy as I am, I stepped on the candles and burnt my foot. It was very embarrassing!

After giving her the wedding gift, I asked Sabeen how many kids we would have; she instantly said that we would have one son, and his name will be Sameer. I was quite surprised and asked her how she could be so sure about this. She told me, "I just am." Today, we have one son, and his name is Sameer.

In the following chapter, we list recipes that are firm favourites at Pakistani weddings - some of these we enjoyed during our wedding.

Makhani Mutton Karahi

MAIN

This was invented by Sabeen while experimenting with different flavours and using different traditional cooking pots. She was always up for creating new variants of traditional Pakistani cuisine for her clients, and this one had a delicious outcome!

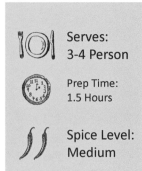

Serves:
3-4 Person

Prep Time:
1.5 Hours

Spice Level:
Medium

INGREDIENTS

- 1 kg Mutton or Lamb (With bones)
- 2-3 Onions (Chopped and grinded)
- 5-6 Tomatoes (Grinded)
- 1 tsp Red Chilli
- 1 tsp Salt
- ½ tsp Turmeric Powder (Haldi)
- ½ tsp Cracked Black Pepper (Grind fresh in the grinder but keep course)
- 1½ tsp Kashmiri Red Chilli
- 1½ tsp Coriander Powder
- 1½ tsp Ginger Garlic Paste
- 1 tsp Cumin Powder

- ¼ tsp Garam Masala
- 1 tsp Red Chilli Flakes
- 1 tsp Dried Fenugreek Leaves
- Chopped Ginger (For garnishing)
- 2 cups Yoghurt (Whisked)
- 3-4 tsp Cream
- 5-6 Green Chillies (2 chillies chopped and rest whole)
- 1 Coriander Bundle (Chopped)
- 3-4 tbsp Sunflower Oil
- 1 tbsp Ghee

METHOD

- Mix meat, onion, tomatoes, two chopped green chillies, all the spices (except fenugreek, garam masala, red chilli flakes and cracked black pepper), ginger garlic paste, add 3-4 cups of water and put on heat. Don't put oil as it will be added later.
- Once the meat is done, then add oil and ghee to a traditional Pakistani clay pot. Bhono extensively till water dries up and the meat smell is gone.
- Then add half yoghurt and bhono, then half yoghurt and bhono.
- Now add fenugreek, red chilli flakes, cracked black pepper, garam masala and three whole green chillies and mix well. Then put on the cover and leave on low heat for 5-10 minutes.
- Once done, then add cream and mix. Then turn off the heat and leave for 2-3 minutes.
- Add chopped coriander, green chillies, finely chopped ginger on top to serve.

Sabeen Secrets:

- Cracked black pepper is key to enhancing the taste, so make sure that you use freshly crushed black pepper.
- Use full cream to have a rich taste.

Shadi Wala Korma (with Gravy/Salan)

SABEEN SIGNATURE/MAIN

Everyone loved Sabeen's 'Shadi Wala Korma' as it was a showstopper. This is my personal favourite. It oozes a rich wedding food aroma, with a dark colour, succulent lamb and hints of cardamom. This mouth-watering Pakistani dish is one of the classics ordered for weddings.

Serves: 4-5 Person

Prep Time: 1.5 Hours

Spice Level: Medium

INGREDIENTS

- 1 kg Chicken (Cut in 12 pieces)
- Crushed Onion (1 Cup)
- 1 cup Yoghurt (Whisked)
- 1½ tsp Ginger Garlic Paste
- 1 tbsp Garam Masala Whole
- 3 Bay Leaves
- 1 tsp Cumin Seeds
- 1 tsp Jaifal Powder (Nutmeg)
- 1 tsp Javatri Powder (Mace)
- 1 tsp Salt
- 1 tsp Red Chilli

- 1 tsp Paprika
- 1½ tsp Coriander Powder
- 1 tsp Cumin Powder
- ½ tsp Turmeric Powder (Haldi)
- ½ tsp Garam Masala Powder
- 1 tsp Butter
- 1 tsp Kewra Water
- 6-8 Cardamom Pods
- 1 tbsp Ginger (Finely chopped)
- 2-3 tbsp Sunflower Oil
- 2 tbsp Ghee

METHOD

- Heat oil and ghee in a pot.
- Add whole garam masala, cumin seeds, and bay leaves. Fry for 1-2 minutes. Then add ginger garlic paste and fry by adding a little water.
- Then add chicken and fry till it changes colour. Cover and cook for 5 minutes.
- Add salt, paprika powder, red chilli, coriander powder, cumin powder and bhono for 2-3 minutes by adding little water in intervals.
- Now turn off the heat and add yoghurt. Then mix well and put the heat on again to bhono till oil separates. Put 1-2 glasses of water to cook the meat.
- Once the chicken is tender, add Jaifal and javitri powder. Bhono for 2-3 minutes.
- Add crushed onions, cardamom pods and mix well. Cook for another 2-3 minutes.
- Now add garam masala powder, butter and kewra powder. Mix well.
- Add ginger on top to serve.

Sabeen Secrets:

- Make sure chicken is not overcooked; else, it will break from the bones.
- Cardamom is the main element of this dish, so it should be visible when serving.
- The cooked dish should have oil as the first layer since this represents the real Shadi Wala Korma.

Signature Lamb Sindhi Biryani

MAIN

If there is one dish in Sabeen's repertoire that you MUST try to make, it is her Sindhi Biryani. This is a special meat and rice dish originating from the time of the Mughals in the early 16th century. This is a version of Biryani originating from Sindh - a province in the south of Pakistan. The tender lamb and potatoes, rich with spices and complemented by Basmati Rice, will make you fall in love again and again. This was very popular on our market stalls.

 Serves:
4-5 Person

 Prep Time:
1.5 Hours

 Spice Level:
Medium

INGREDIENTS

- 1 kg Lamb (Cut in small pieces with bone)
- 1 kg Basmati Rice (4 cups/soaked for 30 minutes)
- 2 Potatoes (Cut in 4 pieces each)
- 3 Onions (Finely chopped)
- 3 Tomatoes (2 chopped, 1 sliced)
- 2 tsp Ginger Garlic Paste
- 8 Dried Aloo Bukhara (Soaked)
- 2 tsp Garam Masala Powder
- 1 Coriander Bundle (Chopped)
- ½ Mint Bundle (Chopped)
- 4-5 Green Chillies (Finely chopped)
- 4-5 Green Chillies (Whole)
- ½ tsp Kewra

- 1 cup Yoghurt (Whipped)
- 2 tsp Red Chilli
- 1 tsp Food Colour (Orange)
- 3 tsp Salt
- 1 tsp Cracked Black Pepper (Grind fresh in the grinder but keep course)
- 2 tsp Coriander Powder
- 1 tsp Cumin Powder
- 5-6 Green Cardamom
- 1 Cinnamon Stick
- 3-4 tbsp Sunflower Oil
- 1 tbsp Ghee

Sabeen's Green Raita:

- 1 Coriander Bundle (Roughly chopped)
- 3-4 Mint Strands (Roughly chopped)
- 1 tsp Sugar

- ½ tsp Salt
- ½ tsp Pepper
- 2 Cup Yoghurt (Whisked)

- Blend all ingredients (except Yoghurt). Once well blended, add to the yoghurt and then mix together.

METHOD

- Fry onion till golden brown and remove half the onion for later.
- In the same oil, add ginger-garlic paste, finely chopped green chillies and tomatoes to fry.
- Then add lamb and all the spices. Bhono by adding small portions of water in intervals.
- Add aloo bukhara and bhono till oil separates, and the lamb smell is gone.
- Add yoghurt and bhono.
- Then add water to cook the lamb and cover the lid at medium heat till lamb is tender.

- Then add potatoes and keep cooking till lamb is fully cooked and oil separates from the masala/gravy. Keep enough gravy since we need to use it, later on to spread on the rice.
- Boil water in a pot with bay leaves, cinnamon stick. Add Kewra, some oil, 2 tsp salt and cardamom. Once water is boiling, add rice. Keep checking since you only want it to be 1 Kanee done.
- Once the rice is 1 kanee, remove it from

heat and drain it thoroughly.

- Now it's time to layer the biryani; brush some ghee at the bottom of the large pot, and then add the first layer of rice. On top of the rice, spread the cooked lamb with some gravy, chopped coriander and mint, as well as tomato slices. Then put the second layer of rice. On the top, sprinkle food colour, ghee, chopped coriander, chopped mint and whole green chillies vertically pushed into the rice and brown onion.
- Cover the lid tightly and leave on very slow heat to cook for 40-45 minutes (Dum) till the rice is done (not mushy but separate and cooked).
- Mix from the sides, bringing it towards the centre. This will help mix the rice nicely with all the ingredients.

Sabeen Secrets:

- Make sure that rice does not overcook when boiling initially or on Dum.
- If the rice is still undone after 45 minutes, then sprinkle come warm water on top and put on dum again for 15 minutes.
- Enjoy it with Sabeen's delicious green raita.

In Pakistan, the wedding is followed by a dinner called "Valima". This is where the groom invites people for dinner and dresses in a suit. These are all traditions that we followed to the dot during our wedding. Sabeen looked as ravishing as usual, and I was so proud to be her husband.

Chicken White Karahi

MAIN

This is a twist on the original Karahi, which is usually red in colour due to the addition of tomatoes. Also, this recipe is very light and delicious, with a very punchy taste profile due to the addition of lemon juice.

Serves:
3-4 Person

Prep Time:
45 Minutes

Spice Level:
Low

INGREDIENTS

Marinate:

- 1 kg Chicken
- 1 tsp Red Chilli
- 1 tsp Ginger Garlic Paste
- 1 tsp Cumin Powder
- 1 tsp Black Pepper
- 2 tsp Yoghurt
- 1 tsp Cinnamon Powder
- 1 tsp White Pepper
- ½ tsp Turmeric
- ½ tsp Garam Masala Powder
- ½ tsp Salt

Gravy:

- 2-3 Green Chillies (Pureed)
- 6-8 Green chillies (Whole)
- ½ Coriander Bundle
- 1 tsp Dry Fenugreek
- 1 tsp Salt
- 1 tbsp Lemon Juice
- 2 tbsp Oil
- 1 tsp Ghee

METHOD

- Marinate the chicken with all ingredients and leave for 1 hour in the fridge.
- Now add ghee and oil to a pot and fry the marinated chicken for 10 minutes.
- Close the pot with a lid and cook for 10 minutes.
- Now add chillies, fenugreek, salt and 1 tbsp lemon juice. Cook for another 5 minutes till the chicken is completely cooked.
- Remove from heat and sprinkle coriander on top for garnish.

Sabeen Secrets:

- Don't cook the chicken for too long since the meat can come off the bones and will become mushy.

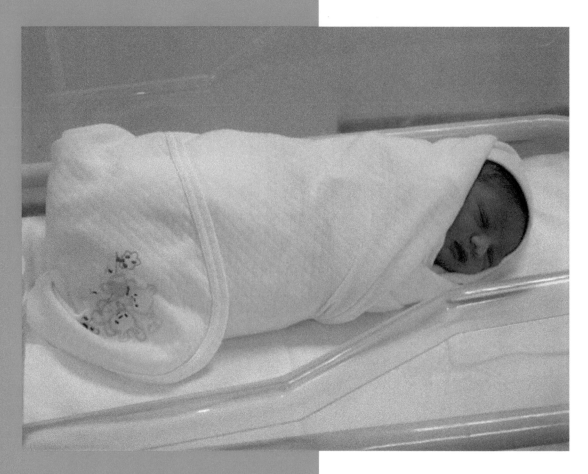

After our wedding festivities had ended ten days later, I went back to Dubai to get the visa formalities arranged, and Sabeen eventually joined me in September with her two Siamese cats Juliet and Sugar; that was her pre-condition to living with me.

We started our life as a young couple (I was 26 and Sabeen was 27), living in a small apartment in Dubai, grasping the world with enthusiasm, our dreams and a lot of fun along the way! From the beginning, we always felt that we were enough for each other, and all we really needed was each other rather than anyone else. We made many friends, but our real enjoyment was spent in the company of each other.

Sabeen was a very humble person and, despite her rich background, never asked me to arrange things just for her comfort. She believed that I would do everything in my control to keep her comfortable and happy. This remained her demeanour throughout our life together. We also always remained friends more than husband and wife, which kept our bond strong and long-lasting. We got many compliments on this throughout our married life, even after 17 years of marriage.

Shortly after, Sabeen became pregnant. It was such great news that I shared it straight away with our parents, who were overjoyed. Especially my parents as our child would be the first grandchild in the family.

We were very careful with Sabeen's pregnancy as we were young parents to be and had no idea what to expect. We didn't have the luxury of having extended family around us, so we had to manage everything ourselves. In the last two months of her pregnancy, Sabeen's parents came to stay with us to help out before and after birth.

Sameer came into the world on June 11, 2005, at around 11 am through a natural delivery. I was there for her throughout and can never forget how Sameer looked right and left after arriving before he started crying. Sabeen felt weak afterwards and had naturally been through a lot of pain, but she was okay, and that's what really mattered. I was so relieved.

This experience impacted me, and I told Sabeen that I would never put her through this pain again since I could not even imagine how she did it. Also, I was always worried about losing Sabeen and didn't want to take any risks – not knowing at the time that I will eventually lose her to Covid-19 and would not be able to do anything about it.

Sabeen decided that she didn't want to work. She wanted to be there to raise Sameer herself, to put in her own efforts and be there for him 24/7 while I was busy at work. We worked together as a team, raising Sameer and taking care of his needs. We never thought about the deep responsibility of it; we just wanted to take care of each other and our son. This made our life much better and our love even stronger for each other.

We lived and raised our son in Dubai for ten years, during which we also witnessed the creation of Burj Khalifa – the tallest skyscraper in the world. We loved living in Dubai and have many beautiful memories there.

Any parent will know that raising a child is tough yet rewarding work! Here are some quick recipes for busy people that can be easily prepared but still have the delicious taste of Sabeen's cuisine.

Aloo Cutlets

SNACK

A simple yet very tasty snack that can be served at parties, gatherings, and events

INGREDIENTS

- 3 Large Potatoes
- 1 Small Onion (Chopped)
- 2 tbsp Coriander Leaves
- ½ tsp Chat Masala
- ¼ tsp Cumin Powder
- Salt (As per taste)
- ½ tsp Red Chilli
- 1 Egg (Whisked for frying)
- Breadcrumbs

Serves:
4 Person

Prep Time:
35 Minutes

Spice Level:
Low

METHOD

- Place the potatoes in a pan and boil it till it becomes soft. Allow to cool, then peel the potatoes and transfer to a medium bowl.
- Use a potato masher to mash them until no large lumps remain. Now add all the ingredients except the egg in the bowl.
- Using your hands, shape the mixture into a flat round patty. You should have 10 to 12 patties. Place the egg and breadcrumbs in shallow bowls so that you can dip them as you cook.
- Heat a large skillet over medium to high heat. Add enough oil to lightly coat the bottom of the pan. Dip both sides of each patty in egg wash and breadcrumbs.
- Place 4-5 patties in the pan and allow them to cook for 3-4 mins on each side using the spatula to turn them.
- Reduce heat as necessary. Remove from the pan and place it on a plate lined with a paper towel to absorb extra oil. Transfer to a serving plate and serve with chutney or raita.

Bhindi (Okra) Kee Sabzee

MAIN

Bhindi (or Okra) is one of the vegetables in Pakistani cuisine that people relish eating alone! Bhindi usually goes well with Masoor Daal and Naan/Chapati.
This dish takes Bhindi to another level. We seldom made Bhindi Kee Sabzee at home since Sameer was not a fan and Sabeen was not keen on eating it on its own. But her clients loved this dish when she made it for her weekly tiffins.

INGREDIENTS

- 500 gms Pre-Cut Frozen Okra
- 2 Onions (Chopped finely)
- 1 tsp Salt
- ¼ tsp Turmeric Powder (Haldi)
- 1 Green Chilli (Chopped)
- 1 tsp Red Chilli Powder
- 1 tsp Cumin Powder
- 1 tsp Coriander Powder
- 1 tsp Ginger Garlic Paste
- 3 cups Oil

Serves:
2 Person

Prep Time:
45 Minutes

Spice Level:
Low

METHOD

- Fry bhindi in 1 tsp of oil for 5-10 minutes till the stickiness disappears in a wok or pan. It's important that the stickiness is gone.
- Add remaining oil in a pot and then add chopped onions to sauté.
- Add tomatoes and bhono till tomatoes become soft.
- Add all spices and bhono by adding a small amount of water till oil separates.
- Add fried bhindi, green chillies and bhono.
- Cover the pot and leave on a very low flame for 5 minutes.

Sabeen Secrets:

- If you are using fresh okra, make sure you wash it and dry it completely before frying. Otherwise, it will become very sticky.

Palak Paneer

MAIN

One of the few vegetarian dishes that Sabeen's customers liked to have in their tiffins. We never had it at home since there were not many takers. This is a dish with a beautiful smooth texture and rich, healthy gravy. Paneer makes it fulfilling and creates a delicious contrast.

INGREDIENTS

- 1 kg Frozen Spinach
- 1 cup Double Cream
- 1 cup Milk
- ½ tsp Salt
- 200 gm Paneer (Fried to golden)
- 1 ½ tsp Ginger Garlic Paste
- 1 tsp Red Chilli
- 1 tsp Cumin Seeds
- 1 Onion (Pureed)
- ½ tsp Turmeric Powder (Haldi)
- 1 tsp Coriander Powder
- 1 tsp Cumin Seeds
- 1 tsp White Pepper
- 2 tbsp Sunflower Oil
- 1 tsp Ghee

Serves:
3-4 Person

Prep Time:
35-40 hour

Spice Level:
Low

METHOD

- Boil water and add frozen spinach and tomatoes to it. Once it's boiled, please put it in the blender and also add a little remaining water from the pot to make a smooth paste texture.
- Heat oil and ghee in a pot. Then add cumin seeds to fry for 1 minute.
- Then add onion to fry, along with ginger garlic paste. Fry till colour turns transparent.
- Now add all spices (except salt) and bhono till oil separates. After this, add salt.
- Now add spinach paste to the pot and mix well. Cook for 5-10 minutes and stir frequently.
- Then add cream and mix well. Then add garam masala and mix again.
- Finally, add fried paneer to the pot, mix well, so the paneer is covered with the gravy and then cover the pot. Leave to cook for 2-3 minutes.
- Serve in a traditional clay dish.

Sabeen Secrets:

- You can also use 100 gms of butter if you don't have double cream.

Tala Gosht (Fry Gosht)

MAIN

My Mum used to make this dish when we were growing up. It came from her roots in Hyderabad, Deccan. Sabeen learnt this recipe after our marriage so I could continue to enjoy it. Although this dish was our family favourite, Sabeen never made it for her clients. I never know why! This is the most simple and tasty Pakistani dish that anyone can enjoy and is best served with Masoor Daal (Red Lentils) and Rice. Don't forget to squeeze lemon juice on top.

 Serves:
3-4 Person

 Prep Time:
1 hour

 Spice Level:
Medium

INGREDIENTS

- 1 kg Boneless Lamb or Beef (Cut into very small pieces)
- 1 Chopped Onion
- 1 tsp Red Chilli
- 1 tsp Salt
- ½ tsp Turmeric Powder (Haldi)
- 1½ tsp Ginger Garlic Paste
- 2 Green Chillies (Chopped)
- 1 Coriander Bundle (Chopped)
- ½ Lemon
- 3-4 tbsp Sunflower Oil

METHOD

- In a pot, add meat, all spices and ginger garlic paste. Mix well and leave for 10 minutes.
- Then add water and boil on medium heat. It should take 45 minutes to 1 hour to cook.
- Once the meat is cooked and water dries up, then add oil in intervals, chopped onion, chopped green chillies and bhono well to remove the smell of meat. This will also enhance the taste of the dish.
- Squeeze lemon and mix well.
- Add chopped coriander, green chillies, finely chopped ginger on top to serve.

Sabeen Secrets:

- Don't worry. This is the whole recipe, and we have not left anything out!
- Always serve with Sabeen's special Tarka Daal and white rice.

DHABA STYLE CHANA DAAL

MAIN

Pakistan is full of street vendors and makeshift food shops (dhabas), where taste rules over experience. We used to sneak out together during our university days to have this Daal and Anda Ghotala (an egg-based, masala-filled dish specialised by Karachi dhabas). You might be sitting next to a road but find yourself immersed in the delicious taste these dhabas produce. Sabeen was always inspired by their style of cooking and merged it with her own expertise to bring this hearty and comforting dish. It is sufficient on its own along with naan.

INGREDIENTS

- 500 gms Chana Daal (Washed and soaked for 2 hours in 1-litre water)
- 1 Onion (Finely chopped)
- 1 tbsp Whole Cumin Seeds
- 1½ tsp Ginger Garlic Paste
- 1 tbsp Tomato Paste
- 1 tsp Cumin Powder
- 1 tsp Red Chilli
- 1 tsp Salt
- 1½ tsp Coriander Powder
- ½ tsp Turmeric Powder (Haldi)
- ½ tsp Garam Masala
- 4 Green Chillies (Whole)
- 1 Coriander bundle (Chopped)
- 2-3 tbsp Ghee

Serves:
2-3 Person

Prep Time:
1,5 hour

Spice Level:
Medium

METHOD

- Place the soaked daal on medium heat for 1 hour. Please keep checking till the daal is done but also retains its shape. Drain and set aside.
- In a pot, heat ghee and then add onions. Fry onion till golden brown, add cumin seeds and ginger garlic paste. Now fry for 2-3 minutes.
- Then add tomato paste and bhono till oil separates.
- Then add coriander, haldi, red chilli, cumin powder and bhono by adding little water.
- Once the oil separates from the masala, then add salt and garam masala. Also, add green chillies at this stage. Add ½ cup water and cover to cook for 5 minutes.
- Now add daal in this gravy and well. Add ½ cup water and now let it cook for 5 minutes by covering the lid.
- Serve with a garnish of fresh coriander, two blobs of butter and thinly sliced ginger.

Sabeen Secrets:

- Ensure that daal is not overcooked when boiling. It should retain its shape and yet be soft before adding to the gravy.

CHICKEN MASALA CURRY

MAIN

One of the staples of any Pakistani household is this classic Chicken Curry. Sabeen made it with ten of her favourite hand-ground spices. What else can you wish for?

INGREDIENTS

- 1 kg Chicken with Bone (Cut in 12 pieces)
- 2 Onions (Fried and crushed)
- 2 Small Tomatoes (Chopped)
- 1½ tsp Ginger Garlic Paste
- 1 tsp Salt
- 2 tsp Red Chilli
- 1 tsp Kashmiri Chilli
- 1 tsp Cracked Black Pepper (Grind fresh in the grinder but keep course)
- ½tsp White Pepper Powder
- 1½ tsp Coriander Powder
- 1 tsp Cumin Powder
- ½ tsp Turmeric Powder (Haldi)
- ¼ tsp Garam Masala Powder
- 1 cup Yoghurt (Whisked)
- 2 Green Chilies (Chopped)
- Finely Chopped Ginger (Few strands for garnishing)
- 3-4 tbsp Sunflower Oil
- 1 tsp Ghee

Serves:
5-6 Person

Prep Time:
1 hour

Spice Level:
Medium

METHOD

- Heat oil and ghee in a pot.
- Add chicken and fry on medium flame till colour changes.
- Add all spices, tomatoes and bhono, adding a little water in intervals. This will stop spices from burning.
- Then add yoghurt and bhono till the oil separates.
- Once the smell of meat is gone, add 3-4 glasses of water and cook on medium heat for 25-30 minutes till meat is cooked.
- Once the meat is cooked, and oil separates, add crushed onions and green chillies. Leave 5-10 minutes to cook.
- Add chopped coriander and few strands of ginger on top to present a colourful dish.

Sabeen Secrets:

- Make sure chicken meat does not come off the bone while frying.
- The gravy should smooth and a little runny rather than pasty.

The element of surprise was a hallmark of our strong relationship; it was what kept us loving each other and feeling young. Once on Sabeen's birthday, I arrived back early from an official meeting in Egypt and went directly to the car showroom to pick up our newly purchased Purple Nissan Tiida. I took it home to Sabeen as her present. She was ecstatic and immediately wanted to drive the car.

In Dubai, we also adopted our cat, Sky. Sabeen always wanted a white cat with blue eyes, which obviously was not easy to find. Sky came to us while living in a villa in Jumeirah Village, where she would come each day to ask for food. Both Sabeen and Sameer would invite her in during the day when I was at the office and then let her out before I came home since they knew I would not be happy to have a cat inside our house until we knew she was vaccinated. I was always surprised as to why this cat was sitting near our window outside, asking to come in! I never figured out what was happening until I was told what was going on behind my back. Eventually, we adopted Sky, and she has been part of our family ever since. As you will notice, she is a white cat with blue eyes.

And Sky was in love with Sameer:

After ten years of living in Dubai, we felt that we needed a change, and we moved to Singapore. While Sameer and I settled in well, Sabeen did not. She was very patient but after almost two years told me that she did not feel happy. Her feelings were enough reason for me to request a transfer to the US or UK. We eventually came to the UK (which Sabeen was keener on), and we were all very happy.

Sabeen was always fascinated with Paris, often requesting me to take her there when I travelled for work. We eventually went in 2018 to both Paris and Barcelona. What a beautiful trip that was!

The next few recipes highlight the international inspiration Sabeen picked up during our travels. This provided global variety to her repertoire.

CHICKEN CORN SOUP

SNACK

This is a very common dish in Pakistani households during winter. I just loved how Sabeen made this soup, which was a perfect starter for all the other delicious dishes that came afterwards. Sabeen's version is very satisfying and comforting.

INGREDIENTS

- ½ kg Chicken (With bones)
- 1 Onion (Small)
- 1 tbsp Ginger (Chopped)
- 1 tbsp Garlic (Chopped)
- 1 tsp Salt
- 7-8 Black Pepper Corns
- 1-2 Cinnamon Stick
- 4-5 Clove
- 2 Litres of Water
- 2-3 tbsp Soya sauce
- 4 tbsp Cornflour (Dissolved)
- 2 Eggs (Whites only)
- 1½ cup Boiled Shredded Chicken
- 1 tsp Black Pepper
- 1 cup Corn (Boiled and coarsely crushed)
- ½ cup Spring Onion (Chopped)

Serves:
4-5 Person

Prep Time:
35-40 Minutes

Spice Level:
Low

METHOD

- In a saucepan, add chicken, onion, black peppercorn, cinnamon stick, cloves, salt, ginger, garlic and water. Bring it to a boil, then let it cook for 45 minutes on low flame.
- Strain the stock and remove chicken pieces. Finely shred the chicken pieces.
- Chop the boiled corn coarsely in a chopper.
- Now bring the stock to boil and add chopped corn and shredded chicken and mix well.
- Add crushed black pepper and soy sauce and cook on low flame for 4-5 minutes.
- Dissolve cornflour in water and whisk well.
- Add cornflour and mix gently. Cook until soup becomes thick.
- Turn off the flame and add egg whites and mix gently.
- Garnish with spring onion, corns, black pepper and soy sauce.

Sabeen Secrets:

- Always garnish the soup with spring onions to give it a nice look and a great aftertaste.

SWEET AND SOUR CHICKEN

MAIN

This dish combines sweet, spicy, salty, and sour – all of Sabeen's favourite flavours in one dish, and it's perfect for a quick lunch or dinner preparation. The chicken is tender and is drenched in flavours that enable this combination. Tasty as it gets!

Serves:
3-4 Person

Prep Time:
35 minutes

Spice Level:
Low

INGREDIENTS

- 3 tbsp Sunflower Oil
- 500 gm Chicken (Boneless)
- 1 tsp Baking Powder
- 5 tbsp All-Purpose Flour
- 2 tbsp Cornflour
- ½ tsp Red Chilli Powder
- 1 tsp Salt
- 1 tsp Black Pepper
- ½ tsp White Pepper
- 1 Egg Whites
- 6 tbsp Chilled Water

Gravy

- 4-5 Garlic Cloves (Finely chopped)
- 2 Medium Onions (Cut in cubes)
- 2 Capsicums (Cut in cubes)
- 2-3 tbsp Cornflour (Dissolved)
- 2 tbsp Oil
- 1 tbsp Vinegar
- 2 tbsp Dark Soy Sauce
- ½ cup Tomato Ketchup
- ½ tsp Red Chilli Powder
- ½ tsp Black Pepper
- 4 tbsp Sugar
- ½ tsp Sesame Seeds (For garnish) (Optional)

METHOD

- Marinate the chicken with red chilli powder, black pepper, white pepper and keep it aside for half an hour.
- Mix all-purpose flour, baking powder, cornflour, salt, egg white and chilled water. Mix well.
- Dip the marinated chicken in the batter and fry for 5-6 minutes on medium to high flame.
- Sauté onion and capsicum for 2-3 minutes in a wok and keep it aside.
- In the same pan, heat the oil and sauté garlic for few minutes, then add tomato ketchup, dark soy sauce, vinegar, sugar and black pepper and mix well.
- Then add chicken and cornflour and cook until the sauce becomes thick.
- Then add onion, capsicum and mix well.
- Sprinkle sesame seeds to garnish.
- Serve it with noodles or rice.

STIR FRY VEGETABLE NOODLES

MAIN

This was a firm favourite among Sabeen's clients. It is packed with flavours, and you can customize the ingredients as you please. In one of the huge parties, she catered to, the first dish to run out was her stir fry vegetable noodles.

INGREDIENTS

- 3 Carrots (Thinly sliced)
- 1 Green and Red Capsicum (Thinly sliced)
- ½ cup Mushrooms
- ½ cup Spring Onion
- 1 cup Green Peas (Frozen)
- 1 tbsp Dark Soy Sauce (or 2 tbsp Light Soya Sauce)
- 1 tbsp Oyster Sauce
- 1 tsp Brown Sugar
- 1 tbsp Vinegar
- 1tbsp Cornflour
- 200 gm Beansprouts
- 1 tsp Salt
- 5-6 Garlic Cloves (Chopped)
- 1½ tsp Black Pepper
- 300 gm Spaghetti
- 4 tbsp Sunflower Oil

Serves: 3-4 Person

Prep Time: 35 minutes

Spice Level: Low

METHOD

- Boil the spaghetti and keep them aside. Keep one cup of water from these while draining.
- Take a bowl and mix dark soy sauce, oyster sauce, vinegar and brown sugar.
- Take a wok and heat the oil, add chopped garlic and sauté for few minutes. Then add carrots, bean sprouts, peas, capsicum and mushroom. Add black pepper and stir fry for 3-4 minutes on medium to high flame.
- Then add the mixture of soy sauce to it and mix well. Add half a cup of noodle water and let it cook for 2-3 minutes.
- Garnish it with spring onions and serve hot.

Sabeen Secrets:

- She used spaghetti instead of egg noodles to give it a different look and a firmer texture.
- Make sure that noodles are not very dry; else, the flavour will be lost. So have enough sauce in it.

Chicken Shawarma Wraps

SNACK

This is the jewel of Middle Eastern cuisine, a truly universal dish that you can find in almost all countries. To us, this represented our time in Dubai, where we started our married life and our family. It is made of meat cut into thin slices, usually grilled in a vertical position in front of a burning rotisserie. However, Sabeen made it in a frying pan, infusing the same spices into chicken strips. With her spices, she was able to closely match the taste profile. Bravo Sabeen!

INGREDIENTS

- ½ kg Chicken Boneless
- 1 tsp Ginger Garlic Paste
- 1 tsp Paprika
- 6 tbsp Yoghurt
- ½ tsp Black Pepper
- ½ tsp All Spice Powder
- 1 tsp Salt
- ¼ tsp Turmeric
- Pita Bread

Yoghurt Sauce:
- 1 cup Greek Yoghurt
- ½ tsp Cumin
- 1 tsp Garlic (Chopped)
- 1 tsp Lemon Juice
- Salt and Pepper (As per taste)
- 2 tsp Oil
- Cucumber, Onion, and Tomato (Sliced)

Serves:
2-3 Person

Prep Time:
1,5 Hours

Spice Level:
Low

METHOD

- First, marinate the chicken with all the spices and leave for an hour. Make the yoghurt sauce by mixing all the ingredients.
- Take a pan put 2 tbsp oil and cook chicken until tender on medium flame.
- Toast the pita wrap. Now assemble the wraps by putting chicken, veggies and yoghurt sauce.
- Serve with pickled cucumbers and yoghurt sauce.

STIR FRY CHICKEN AND VEGETABLE NOODLES

MAIN

This is a dish that contains saucy noodles, crisp hot vegetables, and tender bites of chicken tossed together in this easy stir fry. Sabeen's recipe is packed with oriental flavours and a fragrant aroma.

INGREDIENTS

- 300 gm Chicken (Cut in thin strips)
- 1 tbsp Dark Soy Sauce
- 1 tbsp Oyster Sauce
- 1 tsp Brown Sugar
- 1 tbsp Vinegar
- 1tbsp Cornflour
- 200 gm Beansprouts
- 1 tsp Salt
- 1 tsp Crushed Red Chilli
- 5-6 Garlic Cloves (Chopped)
- 3 Carrots (Thinly sliced)
- 1 Green and Red Capsicum (Thinly sliced)
- ½ Cup Mushrooms
- ½ cup Spring Onion
- 300 gm Egg Noodles
- 4 tbsp Sunflower Oil
- 1½ tsp Black Pepper
- 2 tbsp Fresh Lime Juice

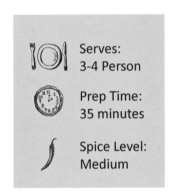

Serves:
3-4 Person

Prep Time:
35 minutes

Spice Level:
Medium

METHOD

- Boil the noodles and keep them aside. Keep one cup of water from these noodles while draining.
- Take a bowl and mix dark soy sauce, oyster sauce, vinegar, brown sugar, cornflour and crushed red chilli.
- In a pan, add oil and fry chicken with salt and pepper for 7-8 minutes. Keep it aside.
- Take a wok and heat the oil, add chopped garlic and sauté for few minutes. Then add carrots, bean sprouts, capsicum and mushroom and stir fry for 3-4 minutes on medium to high flame.
- Then add the mixture of soy sauce to it and mix well. Add chicken, lime juice and half cup noodle water and let it cook for 2-3 minutes.
- Garnish it with spring onions and serve hot.

Mahlabia

DESSERT

This is a famous Arabic sweet milk pudding dessert that is very simple to create and perfect for after-meal desserts. Sabeen loved to make this since it is very fragrant and also included one of her favourite garnishing ingredients, rose petals.

INGREDIENTS

- 4 cups or 1 L whole milk
- 7 tbsp corn starch OR 12 tablespoons rice flour
- 2 tbsp Condensed Milk
- 3 cups Sugar
- 1 tbsp Rose Water
- 1 tsp Cardamom Powder
- Pistachio for garnish (Crushed)
- 1 tsp Dried Rose Petals

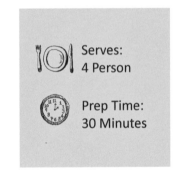

Serves:
4 Person

Prep Time:
30 Minutes

METHOD

- In a pot mix corn starch/rice flour in milk and set aside for 10 minutes.
- Now take a pot and put whole milk, sugar, cardamom powder, condensed milk, rose water and whisk well until dissolved.
- Now add the corn starch mixture to it and whisk again.
- Place pot on low heat and whisk continuously for about 10 minutes until it starts to thicken and obtain a custard consistency. Don't let it boil.
- Remove from heat and leave for 5 minutes.
- Place in small dessert cups and refrigerate for 2-3 hours.
- When ready to serve, garnish with pistachio and rose petals.

LEBANESE CHICKEN STICKS

SNACK

This is another dish which was our favourite during our life in Dubai. Sabeen perfected Middle Eastern spices and flavour profiles by trying several times at home, and of course, we were the beneficiaries every time!

INGREDIENTS

- 1 kg Chicken (Cut in 8 pieces)
- 1 tsp Ground White Pepper
- 1 tsp Salt
- 4 Garlic Cloves (Crushed)
- ½ cup Lemon Juice
- ½ cup Olive Oil

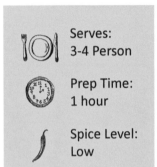

Serves:
3-4 Person

Prep Time:
1 hour

Spice Level:
Low

METHOD

- Preheat oven to 200 degrees centigrade.
- Place chicken in a large tray.
- Sprinkle salt and pepper generously in a bowl mix together garlic, olive oil and lemon. Pour over chicken and cover with foil.
- Stick the chicken on wooden skewers and bake in preheat the oven for 30 mins.
- Now remove the foil and cook for another 10 mins till chicken and potatoes turns golden brown.

Sabeen Secrets:

- Don't overcook the chicken as it needs to remain moist.

VIETNAMESE ROLLS

SNACK

This is a result of our travels in Asia, especially Singapore, Vietnam, and Malaysia. Living in Singapore gave us the opportunity to explore and appreciate Southeast Asian cuisine, and Sabeen learned to make several dishes that became our favourite. This is one such dish that gives an alternative to the Chinese style. Fried spring rolls are made with Rice Vermicelli, which is very thin rice noodles. We loved it!

INGREDIENTS

- 2 tbsp Sugar
- ¼ cup Fish Sauce
- ¼ cup White Vinegar
- 3 ounce Rice Vermicelli
- 1 tbsp Lime Juice
- 1 Garlic Clove (Minced)
- ¼ tsp Red Chilli Flakes
- 8 Shrimps (Large peeled)
- 4 Rice Wrappers
- 1 tbsp Lettuce Leaves (Finely chopped)
- 1 tbsp Mint Leaves (chopped)
- 1 tbsp Thai Basil (chopped)

Serves:
2 Person

Prep Time:
40-45 minutes

Spice Level:
Low

METHOD

- Whisk vinegar, fish sauce, sugar, lime juice, garlic, and red chilli flakes mix and set aside until your dipping sauce is ready.
- Fill a bowl with room temperature water and soak rice vermicelli for 1 hour.
- Transfer rice vermicelli noodles to the pot of boiling water and cook for 1 minute. Remove and drain in a colander. Immediately rinse the vermicelli with cold water, stirring to separate the noodles.
- Bring a large pot of water to a boil. Drop in the shrimp and cook until curled and pink, about 1 minute. Remove the shrimp and drain.
- Slice each shrimp in half lengthwise.
- To assemble the rolls, dip 1 rice wrapper in a large bowl of warm water for 1 minute to soften. Then lay the wrapper flat.
- Place wrapper on a work surface and top with four shrimp halves, ¼ of the chopped lettuce, ½ ounce vermicelli, and ¼ each of the mint and Thai basil.
- Fold the right and left edges of the wrapper over the ends of the filling and roll up the spring roll. Repeat with remaining wrappers and ingredients.
- Cut each roll in half and serve with dipping sauce.

Sabeen Secrets:

- Serve with Hoisin Sauce, don't eat with ketchup!

CHICKEN MANDI
MAIN

We learned to love this dish while living in Dubai. There was a place in Jumeirah that served excellent Lamb and Chicken Mandi, so we always went there to eat it. Traditionally, Mandi is cooked in an underground oven, which gives it a smoky aroma due to the coal. However, we can cook it in our kitchens as well using the recipe we are providing.

 Serves:
5-6 Person

 Prep Time:
2-3 Hours

Spice Level:
Low

INGREDIENTS

- 1 kg Chicken (4 pieces)
- 1 Onion (Finely chopped)
- 1 tbsp Whole Garam Masala
- 2 Pieces of Dry Lemons
- 3-5 Green Cardamom
- 1½ tsp Ginger Garlic Paste
- 1 tsp Salt
- 1 tsp Cracked Black Pepper (Grind fresh in the grinder but keep course)
- 1½ tsp Coriander Powder
- 2 tsp Cumin Powder
- 1 tsp Fennel Seeds
- 1 tsp Ginger Powder
- 1 tbsp Lemon Powder
- 1 tbsp White Cumin Powder

- ½ tsp Turmeric Powder (Haldi)
- ¼ tsp Garam Masala Powder
- 2 Cinnamon sticks
- 2-3 Bay Leaves
- 5-6 Pieces of Cloves
- 1 tbsp Raisins
- ½ Carrot (Cut in strands)
- 1 tsp Yellow Colour
- 1 kg Basmati Rice
- 3 Boiled Eggs (Cut in half)
- 1 cup Peas (Frozen and boiled)
- 1 tbsp Sunflower Oil
- 4 tbsp Ghee

Sabeen's Special Tamatam Kee Chutney:

- 1 Chopped Garlic
- 1-2 Green Chillies (Remove seeds)
- 3-4 Medium Tomatoes (Chopped)
- 1 Small Onion (Chopped)
- ¼ Chopped Parsley
- ¼ tsp Salt
- 2 tsp Olive Oil
- Grind all ingredients together.

METHOD

- Mix all dry spices (except whole garam masala, cardamom and dry lemon) in oil and marinate the chicken for 1 hour.
- Heat half of the ghee, add whole garam masala, green cardamom, and dry lemon and then add chicken to fry.
- Now add water and let the chicken cook. Once it's cooked, separate cooked chicken and stock, which will be used later. You should have at least 3 ½ cups of stock.
- Fry the Onions in the other half of the ghee till golden brown. Now add rice, stock, cinnamon sticks, bay leaves and cloves.
- Cook till it comes to a boil, then reduce the heat to low, cover the lid and cook for 15 minutes.
- After 15 minutes, open the lid and fluff the rice. Then place the chicken on top, add raisins and put on dum for 5-10 minutes till rice is tender.
- Once done, fry carrot in Ghee and then spread on top of the rice to serve.
- Finally, to give a smoky flavour put the burning coal piece in a foil on top of the rice and then put a little oil on it before covering the pot. This will release the smoke quickly.
- Add boiled eggs and peas on the side for presentation.

Sabeen Secrets:

- The most crucial part is to ensure that rice does not get overdone and become slimy. So, ensure that you check while rice is cooking.
- Serve with Sabeen's special Tamatam Chutney.

KUNG PAO CHICKEN

Serves: 4-5 Person

Prep Time: 1.5 Hours

Spice Level: Medium

SABEEN SIGNATURE/ MAIN

This is a highly addictive stir-fried chicken made by Sabeen. It is a perfect combination of salty, sweet, and spicy flavour with mouth-watering Kung Pao Sauce and Large Kashmiri Chillies (Pakistani Chinese Touch).

INGREDIENTS

- 500 gm Chicken (Boneless, cut in small square pieces)
- 6 tbsp Sunflower Oil
- 1 tsp Salt
- 1 Egg (Beaten)
- 1 tsp Cracked Black Pepper
- 1 tbsp Soya Sauce
- 2 tbsp Corn Flour

Marinate the chicken with the above ingredients for 15 minutes and deep fry it for 5-6 minutes in medium heat and keep it aside.

Kung Pao Sauce Prep

- 1½ Onion (Diced)
- 1 tbsp Soy Sauce
- 1½ Capsicum (Diced)
- 1½ Carrot (Diced)
- Spring Onion (Chopped)
- 5-6 Whole Red Long Chilli
- 2-3 Kashmiri Whole Chillies
- Sichuan Peppercorns (Powder)
- 1 tsp Brown Sugar
- 4 tbsp Sunflower Oil

- 2 tbsp Chilli Oil
- 1½ tsp Ginger Garlic Paste
- 1 cup Peanuts
- 4 tbsp Dark Soy Sauce
- 1 tsp Salt
- ½ Cup Water
- 3 tbsp Oyster Sauce
- 4 tbsp Corn Flour (Dissolved in water)

METHOD:

- In a wok, fry the whole red chillies until the colour is changed to deep red or black. Put them aside.
- Take a pan and add oil, chilli oil, brown sugar, and ginger-garlic paste in it. Fry on a medium flame for 3-4 minutes.
- Add vegetables, fried chicken, fried whole red chilli, peppercorn powder and peanuts and toss it well. Then add water and let it cook for few minutes on medium flame.
- Now add dark soy sauce, salt, oyster sauce, Kashmiri chilli and mix well.
- Then add dissolved cornflour, stir well and let it cook until the gravy becomes thick.

Sabeen Secrets:

- The key to a juicy and moist chicken dish is not to over-fry. Watch your timing.

Chilli Chicken

Serves:
3-4 Person

Prep Time:
35-40 minutes

Spice Level:
Medium

SABEEN SIGNATURE/ MAIN

A key part of her Pakistani Chinese menu is Chilli Chicken. The tender chicken boneless strips cooked with fresh vegetables and mouth-watering sauce made people want more.

INGREDIENTS

- 500 gm Chicken (Boneless)
- 4 tbsp Sunflower Oil
- 1 tbsp Sesame Seeds
- 2-3 tbsp Soy Sauce
- 1 tsp Salt
- ½ tsp Sugar
- 1 tsp Black Pepper
- 4-5 Garlic Cloves (Chopped)
- 3 tbsp Corn Flour (Water dissolved)
- 6 Green Chillies (Julienne)
- 2 Capsicum (Cut in medium cubes)
- 1 tsp Hot Sauce
- 1 cup Water

METHOD

- Cut the chicken into strips.
- In a wok, heat oil and add chopped garlic, fry it for few minutes.
- Add chicken and fry it for 10 minutes on high flame.
- Then turn the flame on medium heat and add soy sauce, black pepper, salt and sugar. Mix well and let it cook for few minutes.
- Now add cornflour and cook for 2-3 minutes.
- Add green chilis and capsicum and cook for few minutes on low flame.
- Sprinkle sesame seeds once ready.
- Serve with plain rice.

Sabeen Secrets:

- The key to a juicy and moist chicken dish is not to over-fry. Watch your timing.

UMM-E-ALI

DESSERT

This dessert took back Sabeen to her roots - baking. She loved experimental baking influenced by the diverse exposure of her global travels. This is her twist on Umm-e-Ali, which is the famous Arabic version of bread and butter pudding. The word literally means "Ali's Mother" in Arabic.

INGREDIENTS

- ½ Sheet of Puff Pastry
- 2 Cups Milk
- ½ cup Heavy Cream
- 4 tbsp Sugar
- 50 gms Almonds (Crushed)
- 50 gms Walnuts (Crushed)
- 20 gms Desiccated Coconut
- 1 cup Whip Cream
- 20 gms Raisins

 Serves:
2-3 Person

 Prep Time:
35-40 Minutes

METHOD

- Heat milk, cream, and sugar. Cook till sugar dissolves and then remove.
- Prepare the pastry as per pack instructions. Put it on a lightly oiled baking tray and bake for 15 minutes at 200 degrees Celsius. Remove from oven and allow to cool enough to handle. Then break it into bite-size pieces.
- Taking a baking dish and sprinkle pastry and layer with almonds, walnuts, raisins and desiccated coconut.
- Gently pour milk mixture over it and spread on top.
- Bake in preheated oven at 180 for 20 minutes and remove.
- Sprinkle some raisins on top and serve warm.

ENTREPRENEURIAL FORAY

Sabeen started her entrepreneurial journey with a baking business idea. Utilizing the baking skills, she acquired in her early life and her professional training, without any help she established a website and started promoting her cupcakes. She loved baking and had a natural talent for it. This became what remains of her business today - Pink Oven - which initially focused on baking and baking events.

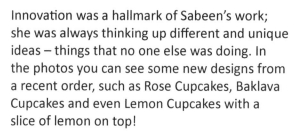

Innovation was a hallmark of Sabeen's work; she was always thinking up different and unique ideas – things that no one else was doing. In the photos you can see some new designs from a recent order, such as Rose Cupcakes, Baklava Cupcakes and even Lemon Cupcakes with a slice of lemon on top!

She also made some super creative cupcakes for special occasions. These truly showed her passion and talent for her business and her skillset:

She had profound love for roses, and she created many beautiful designs for her Rose Cupcakes Line:

...leading to Wedding themed cupcakes:

She also gave classes on cupcakes and cake-toppers making:

PINK OVEN CLASSES

CHRISTMAS TREE & TOPPER CLASS

FUN WORK WITH FONDANT & SUGAR PASTE

SATURDAY · DECEMBER 10, 2016 10 AM-11 AM

VENUE: ORLEANS PARK SCHOOL, TW1 3BB

For Registeration/ Information Email us:
pinkoveninfo@gmail.com
£5 per kid (materials included)
www.pinkoven.co.uk

She also received many corporate orders and completed these with a high degree of skill and professionalism...the clients loved them!

She also made a large cupcake order in Royal Nawab (a famous Pakistani Buffet Restaurant in Perivale, London) on Chand Raat (the night before the Muslim festival of Eid), where she was invited by the organiser specifically because of her great work:

She was very competitive and was always looking for opportunities to display her work. This compelled her to take part in a baking competition, where she came runner-up.

...and ended up being on
the popular Bollywood
entertainment channel,
B4U:

After that mouth-watering introduction to the world's
best cupcakes, let us take you through some of
Sabeen's sweet and delicious recipes for brownies.

Double Chocolate Brownies

DESSERT

Sabeen loved baking and having these. She was very happy creating these heavenly, light, delicious and fluffy brownies for us and her clients. Goes well with tea or coffee.

INGREDIENTS

- 3/4 cup Baking Cocoa
- 1/2 tsp Baking Soda
- 2/3 cup Butter (Melted, Divided)
- 1/2 cup Boiling Water
- 2 cups Sugar
- 2 Large Eggs (Room Temperature)
- 1 1/3 cups All-Purpose Flour
- 1 tsp vanilla extract
- 1/4 tsp Salt
- 2 cups (12 ounces) Semisweet Chocolate Chunks

Serves:
4-5 Person

Prep Time:
35 Minutes

METHOD

- Preheat oven to 180 degrees Celsius.
- In a large bowl, combine cocoa and baking soda. Blend 1/3 cup melted butter. Add boiling water; stir until well blended.
- Stir in sugar, eggs and remaining butter. Add flour, vanilla and salt. Stir in chocolate chunks.
- Pour into a grease a baking pan. Bake 35-40 minutes or until brownies begin to pull away from sides of pan.
- Cool, cut with a sharp knife in nice square and serve.

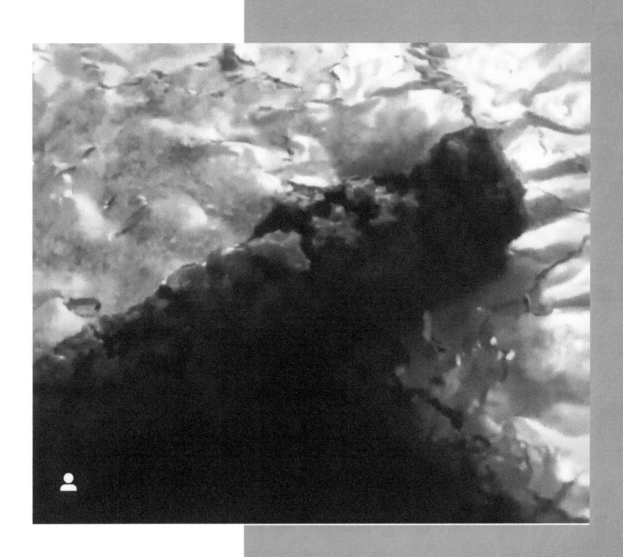

PINKOVEN 2.0

In my professional career I have travelled a lot around the world and met many company leaders and business owners; out of everyone I have come across, I found Sabeen to have one of the sharpest business minds. It was not an easy task to build a successful business ground-up within 3 years of moving to London. She knew what she was doing!

Although Sabeen loved baking, she was always planning and thinking about the future of Pink Oven. She explored various ways to expand the business. Besides being a talented baker, she was also a great cook which started her thinking about expanding into savoury food. Being an astute entrepreneur, she knew that the business could grow significantly if she could launch and popularise Pakistani Cuisine under the Pink Oven umbrella brand. She was also convinced that a little theatre would help her popularity which motivated her to move towards Street Food market stalls. All these measures helped Pink Oven to become very well known and loved by its clients.

Again - all by herself, she re-launched Pink Oven and developed a new website www.pinkoven. co.uk. Her website won the second most liked website on the WIX platform globally.

Her recipes were delicious and high quality. She made all her dishes with premium ingredients and the highest level of hygiene - she was Level 3 HACCP Certified. It was not long before people realised that although she might not be cheap, she was one of the best in the business.

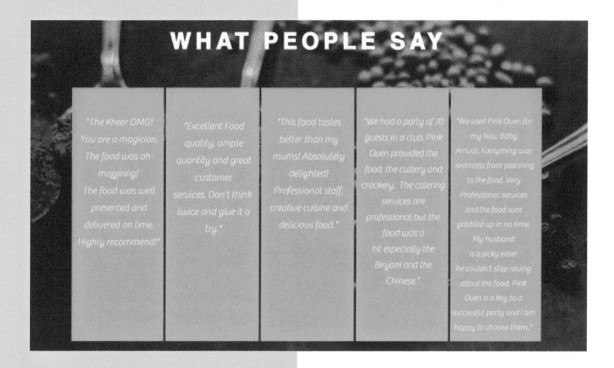

WHAT PEOPLE SAY

"The Kheer OMG! You are a magician. The food was oh-magginng! The food was well presented and delivered on time. Highly recommend!"

"Excellent Food quality, ample quantity and great customer services. Don't think twice and give it a try."

"This food tastes better than my mums! Absolutely delighted! Professional staff, creative cuisine and delicious food."

"We had a party of 70 guests in a club. Pink Oven provided the food, the cutlery and crockery. The catering services are professional but the food was a hit especially the Biryani and the Chinese."

"We used Pink Oven for my New Baby Arrival. Everything was seamless from planning to the food. Very Professional services and the food was gobbled up in no time. My husband is a picky eater he couldn't stop raving about the food. Pink Oven is a key to a successful party and I am happy to choose them."

As they say, "Taste is in the hands". Her personalised touch and attention to detail made her food irresistible. She specialised in Party Food and Pakistani Cuisine in her menus. She used a Halal 5 rated meat supplier to ensure that premium cuts were used in her food preparation. She bought fresh vegetables to ensure quality dishes. She had Level 3 Food hygiene & HACCP certified which meant that hygiene was a religion at Pink Oven. That is why she claimed that the Pink Oven food was Premium, Fresh and Handmade.

She had four clear business revenue streams: Parties, Weekly Tiffins, Corporate Events and Market Stalls.

The following recipes are some of the most sought-after menu items that Sabeen's clients (and of course her family!) always asked for. These will make your family and friends very happy too!

Lamb Nihari

MAIN

This is by far Sabeen's most favourite dish. She always said "Morning Nihari, Afternoon Nihari and Evening Nihari", which basically meant that she could eat Nihari the whole day! We loved the Nihari she made as it had so much passion and love added to it.

 Serves:
5-6 Person

 Prep Time:
3-4 hours

 Spice Level:
High

INGREDIENTS

- 2 kg Lamb Meat with Bones (Cut only in 4 large pieces. Also separately buy bone marrow and bones)
- 4 Onions (Medium Chopped)
- 2 tbsp Red Chilli
- 2 tsp Garam Masala
- 2 tbsp Kashmiri Chilli
- ½ tsp Turmeric Powder (Haldi)
- 1 tsp Black Pepper Corns
- 1 tbsp White Cumin Seeds
- 1 tsp Fennel Seeds
- 10 Cloves
- 6 pieces of Green Cardamom

- 6 Pieces of Black Cardamom
- 4 pieces Bay Leaves
- 4 pieces Cinnamon
- 1 tsp Nutmeg and Mace
- Flour mixed in water (Half cup)
- 1 ½ tsp Ginger Garlic Paste
- 1 tsp Salt
- 1 Chopped Coriander
- 1 Lemon (Cut in Thick Pieces)
- 4 Green Chilies (Coarsely Chopped)
- 2 Ginger (Finely Chopped in Strands)
- 5 tbsp Sunflower Oil

METHOD

- Lightly roast and then grind all whole spices (cloves, black pepper corns, fennel seeds, cinnamon sticks, both cardamoms, bay leaves and white cumin seeds).
- Boil Meat and Bones (till half cooked).
- Heat oil and fry onion till brown. Add ginger garlic paste and meat to bhono well till oil comes up. Take this oil out and keep separate.
- Add all spices and mix well.
- Then add one jug of water and leave on very low heat for 3-4 hours.
- Once meat is done, add prepared flour in water in intervals while stirring with a spoon. Make sure it mixes well and don't add all flour water in one go.
- Now add bone marrow and leave for 10-15 on very low heat.
- Once done, add Kashmiri chilli powder in the oil kept separately and fry for 3-4 minutes. Then pour this oil on top, along with chopped coriander, lemon, finely chopped ginger and chopped green chillies to serve.

Sabeen Secrets:

- Always keep a separate plate of chopped coriander, lemon, finely chopped ginger and chopped green chillies as people would add it while taking second helpings.
- The more the Nihari cooks, the more taste it will give.
- You can also add brain in Nihari if you like.
- Eat with Naan (Or rice as I would always do).

Pakora Karhi

MAIN

This is a unique, tangy and flavourful Pakistani dish. You can have it with minced meat curry and rice or only with rice. The combination of soft, moist pakoras with daal consistency curry and the inviting mustard/yellow colour makes this a must try from Sabeen's cuisine.

 Serves:
5-6 Person

 Prep Time:
1.5 hours

 Spice Level:
Medium

INGREDIENTS

Curry Mixture:

- 1 kg Yoghurt
- 9 tsp Gram Flour (Sieved)
- ½ tsp Red Chilli
- 1 ½ tsp Ginger Garlic Paste
- ½ tsp Turmeric Powder (Haldi)
- 1 tsp Salt

For Pakoras (Gram Flour Dumplings):

- 1 cup Gram Flour (Sieved)
- 1 ½ tsp Red Chilli
- ¾ tsp Salt
- ½ tsp Turmeric
- 1 tsp Baking Soda
- Add warm water (little at a time) till it becomes a smooth paste. Leave for at least 10 minutes.

Tarka:

- 1 tbsp Ghee
- 3 tbsp Sunflower Oil
- 1 Onion (Finely Sliced)
- 1 tsp Curry Leaves
- 4-5 Long Dried Red Chillies
- 1 tsp Zeera

METHOD

- Mix all curry ingredients in a blender with 1 cup water.
- Then put oil and ghee in a pot, add some curry leave and fry for 1 minute. Then add curry mixture, 3-4 cups of warm water and cook while continuously stirring it on medium heat. Dont stop stirring else there will be lumps in the curry.
- Once it comes to boil and smell of gram flour is gone, lower the heat and cover it with a lid to cook for 60 minutes till curry become thick (ensure there are no lumps).
- Deep fry the Pakoras in hot oil till golden brown and then take out on a kitchen towel to absorb excess oil. Then soak in warm water to make these soft 10-15 minutes.
- Add fried pakoras in the curry mixture.
- For Tarka, fry onion in a pan till golden brown. Then add all other ingredients and fry for 1-2. Now pour over the Pakora Curry you just prepared.
- Serve with white basmati rice

Sabeen Secrets:

- Make sure there are no lumps in the curry. It needs to be smooth as a criminal!
- Curry needs to be cooked long and slow to get the right consistency and flavour. Don't rush it.
- Curry leaves is the end game and a must have in the Tarka to get the right flavour combination.

Shimla Mirch Keema (Chicken)

MAIN

This simple yet delicious dish frequently made its way into Sabeen's weekly tiffin menu. She got a lot of feedback from her clients that their entire family loved it!

Serves:
3-4 Person

Prep Time:
1 hour

Spice Level:
Low

INGREDIENTS

- 1 kg Chicken Breast Mince
- 1 Onion (Finely Chopped)
- 2 Pieces Shimla Mirch/Bell Pepper (Remove seeds and chop in medium pieces)
- 1 ½ tsp Ginger Garlic Paste
- 1 tsp Salt
- 1 tsp Red Chilli

- 1 ½ tsp Coriander Powder
- 1 tsp Cumin Powder
- ½ tsp Turmeric Powder (Haldi)
- Chopped Coriander
- 4 Green Chilies (2 whole and 2 chopped)
- 3-4 tbsp Sunflower Oil
- 1 tsp Ghee

METHOD

- Heat Oil in a Pot and add onions to sauté.
- Add chicken mince and ginger garlic paste. Fry a little till colour changes.
- Add all spices and bhono adding a little water in intervals. This will stop spices from burning. Make sure chicken mince smell is gone.
- Once the smell of meat is gone, add shimla mirch pieces and bhono
- Add green chillies and leave for 5 minutes to cook.
- Add 1 cup water and cover.
- Once water dries up, add chopped coriander and green chilies on top to present a colourful dish.

Sabeen Secrets:

- Don't chop the shimla mirch too small as they need to retain the shape.
- Don't leave any gravy or water in the cooked dish. This is a dry dish, and all spices and juices must soak up to give the needed flavour.

Chicken Fajita Pasta

MAIN

One of the most popular dishes for corporate and private parties. Sabeen loved western cuisine and thus she made this with a lot of passion. It's another matter that we at home preferred Pakistani cuisine for everyday meals. Thus, this was mostly done for clients.

INGREDIENTS

- ½ kg Chicken Breast (Boneless)
- 2 cups Diced Onion
- 2 cups Bell Pepper (Diced)
- 2 tbsp Fajita Seasoning
- 1 cup Chicken Broth
- 2 Garlic (Chopped)
- ½ tsp Salt
- 3 cups Penne Pasta
- 1 cup Double Cream
- 1 cup Shredded Mozzarella Cheese
- ½ cup Chopped Parsley
- 2 tbsp Olive Oil

Fajita Seasoning

- 1 tbsp Corn starch
- 2 tsp Chilli Powder
- 1 tsp Salt
- 1 tsp Paprika
- 1 tsp Sugar
- ½ tsp Garlic Powder
- 1/4 tsp Cayenne Pepper
- ½ tsp Cumin Powder

 Serves:
3-4 Person

 Prep Time:
40-45 minutes

 Spice Level:
Low

METHOD

- Cut chicken into strips and season them with half fajita seasoning. In a pan heat 1 tbsp. olive oil and cook chicken.
- When the chicken is cooked, remove the chicken to the plate.
- In the same pot add the remaining oil and put the veggies and the remaining seasoning and cook for 5 mins on medium flame.
- Now add garlic and cook on low flame for 30 seconds. Remove the veggies and place with chicken.
- Now in the same pan add broth, cream, diced tomatoes, uncooked pasta and salt. Bring it to a boil and then cover and reduce the flame.
- Cook until the pasta is tender. Now add the veggies and chicken.
- Add cheese on top and mix well.
- Add chopped parsley for garnishing.

Sabeen Secrets:

- Make sure that pasta is not overcooked or else it would become hard and chewy.

Chicken Manchurian

MAIN

Another staple in Pakistani Chinese cooking. The dish Sabeen created was sweet and sour, with fried boneless chicken that was very tender. Serve with plain rice or noodles.

INGREDIENTS

- 500 gm Chicken (Cut in Cubes)
- 2 tsp Soy Sauce
- 1 tsp Oyster Sauce
- 1 tsp Vinegar
- 1 tsp Sugar
- 3-4 Garlic Cloves (Finely Chopped)
- 1 tsp Salt
- 2 Carrots (Cut in Thin Slices)
- 1 Green Capsicum (Cut in Small Cubes)
- 1 Onion (Cut in Small Cubes)
- 2 Eggs
- 2 tbsp Corn Flour (Dissolved)
- 2 tbsp Sunflower Oil
- 1/2 tsp Black Pepper

Serves:
3-4 Person

Prep Time:
35 minutes

Spice Level:
Low

METHOD

- In a bowl add chicken, salt, eggs and cornflour mix well and set aside.
- Take a wok and heat oil in it. Once hot, fry chicken pieces until they turn golden. Take it out and keep it aside.
- In the same wok add 2tbsp oil and sauté garlic in it for 2 minutes. Then add onion and fry for few minutes. Now add capsicum, carrots, soy sauce, oyster sauce, sugar, vinegar, salt, black pepper and cook for few minutes. Add water as required.
- Then add the cornflour and cook until the sauce becomes thick.
- Now add the chicken and mix well.
- Best served hot.

Sabeen Secrets:

- You can also make the dish dry which would lock in the flavours in the chicken.
- Don't overcook the chicken since you want the tender, juicy texture.

Dum Ka Keema

MAIN

Another family favourite which Sabeen's clients loved. It is very simple to make yet needs fine balance to achieve the divine taste. It has the oomph factor of smoke, with a subtle coal flavour at the end. Sublime yet flavourful.

 Serves: 3-4 Person

 Prep Time: 1 Hour

 Spice Level: Medium

INGREDIENTS

- 1 kg Lamb Mince (Keema)
- 1tsp Tenderiser
- 2 tsp Sesame Seeds (white)
- 2 tsp Poppy Seeds
- 10 Cloves
- 1 tsp Cumin Seeds
- 2 tsp Coconut Powder
- 2 tsp Coriander Seeds
- 1 ½ tsp Ginger Garlic Paste
- 1 tsp Salt
- 1 tsp Red Chilli
- 1 tsp Black Pepper Corns
- ½ tsp Turmeric Powder (Haldi)
- Chopped coriander
- 2 tbsp Yogurt
- 2 Onions (Finely Chopped)
- 4 Green Chilies (whole)
- 3-4 tbsp Sunflower Oil
- 1 tsp Ghee
- 1 piece of coal for smoking

METHOD

- Roast all whole spices lightly (Cloves, Coconut, Black Peppercorns, Cumin Seeds, Poppy Seeds, Sesame Seeds, Coriander Seeds) and grind them.
- Marinate the lamb mince with roasted spice mix, Ginger Garlic, Yoghurt, tenderiser and all other spice powders. Keep in the fridge overnight.
- Heat oil in a pot and fry onions till golden brown.
- Add marinated mince and mix with onions. Leave it for some time on very low heat to cook through (about 15 minutes). If there is a need, add some water.
- Once cooked, then bhono by adding a little amount of oil.
- Once done, smoke the prepared keema with burning coal and cover the frying pan so the smoke remains inside and infuses into the meat to give a nice smoky smell and taste.
- Garnish with freshly chopped coriander, finely chopped onion rings and whole green chillies.

Sabeen Secrets:

- Put the burning coal piece in a foil on top and then put a little oil on it before covering the frying pan. This will release the smoke quickly.

Mutton Haleem

MAIN

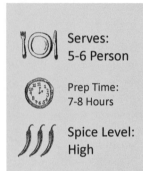

Serves:
5-6 Person

Prep Time:
7-8 Hours

Spice Level:
High

Haleem is a dish of the Moghuls and has always had a very special place in the Pakistani culinary portfolio. It is also a dish that is prepared and served on Islamic New Year (Muharram). Sabeen always loved making Haleem since her clients were always very keen on it. Her Haleem recipe is creamy, thick, and full of flavour.

INGREDIENTS

- 3 kg Mutton or Lamb in large chunks (Also take 250 gm bones separately)
- 1 cup Chana Daal (Soaked Overnight)
- 1 cup Masoor Daal (Soaked Overnight)
- 1 cup Mash Daal (Soaked Overnight)
- ½ kg Wheat (Soaked Overnight)
- 1 tbsp Red Chilli
- 4-5 Onions (For Cooking and Tarka)
- 1 tsp Salt
- ½ tsp Turmeric Powder (Haldi)
- 1 tsp Cracked Black Pepper (Grind fresh in the grinder but keep course)
- 1 ½ tsp Kashmiri Red Chilli

- 1 ½ tsp Coriander Powder
- 1 ½ tsp Ginger Garlic Paste
- 1 tsp Cumin Powder
- ¼ tsp Garam Masala
- 1 tsp Chaat Masala
- 1 tsp Crushed Red Chilli
- Finely chopped ginger for garnishing
- 2-3 Green Chillies (Chopped)
- 1/2 bundle of Coriander (Chopped)
- 1 Lemon (Cut in Thick Slices)
- 1 tbsp Sunflower Oil
- 2 tsp Ghee

METHOD

- Heat oil in a pot and fry onions till brown. Add all spices (except Chaat masala), ginger garlic paste and bhono by adding water in intervals. Then add yoghurt and bhono again till oil comes up.
- Add meat to fry and bhono.
- Then add soaked daals, wheat along with 8-10 cups of water to cook. Cook for at least 5-6 hours on low heat.
- Once the meat is tender/cooked and the mixture becomes like a thick paste but still a bit runny, grind it well.
- Tarka: Heat Ghee in a frying pan and fry onions till golden.
- Pour this Tarka on the Haleem and garnish it with Coriander, Ginger, Chaat Masala, Lemon Slices and Green Chillies.

Sabeen Secrets:

- The more you cook the Haleem, the better the flavours and taste.
- Grinding will create fine threads of meat which is the texture you want in the Haleem.

Dhaba Mash Daal

MAIN

A firm favourite at breakfast, served with Parathas. I used to love having this but Sabeen not so much. However, this Dhaba Style Daal was a regular feature in her tiffin menus

INGREDIENTS

- 500 gms White Lentils (Mash Daal)
- 1 Onion (Medium Sliced)
- 2-3 Tomatoes (Medium Diced)
- 1 tbsp Whole Cumin Seeds
- ½ tsp Garam Masala
- 1 ½ tsp Ginger Garlic Paste
- ¼ tsp Red Chilli Powder
- 1 tsp Salt to taste
- 6-7 Whole Red Chilli
- Few Strands of Ginger (Finely Sliced)
- Few strands of Coriander
- 2-3 Green Chillies (Chopped)

Serves:
3-4 Person

Prep Time:
45 Minutes

Spice Level:
Low

METHOD

- Wash white lentils thoroughly to remove all dirt. Then soak it in water for 1 hour.
- Boil the lentils in hot water and cook till its boils….remove the scum coming on top.
- Add ginger-garlic paste, red chilli, garam masala and salt. Cook on medium heat till the lentil is done and water dries up (about 20 minutes). You should see each lentil piece separately in the pot and not like a mash. Take it out in a bowl.
- Then heat oil, add onion and whole red chillies. Fry till onion gets brown and then add cumin seeds, green chillies and ginger. This is called Dhaba Tarka.
- Pour over the lentils. Also, put some freshly chopped coriander on top.

Sabeen Secrets:

- Eat with fresh parathas.
- Cooked Daal should remain dry as this is the right texture for it.

Vegetable Fried Rice

MAIN

Quick and easy to make. This rice can be a great complement to Sabeen's other sauce based Pakistani Chinese dishes such as Chicken Manchurian, Chicken Chilli or Lamb in Oyster Sauce.

INGREDIENTS

- 500 gms Boiled Basmati Rice
- 2 tsp Garlic Cloves (Finely Chopped)
- 2 tsp Ginger (Finely Chopped)
- 2 Star Anise
- 1 Onion (Chopped Very Small)
- 1 cup Green Beans (Chopped Small)
- 1 cup Cabbage (Chopped Small)
- 1 cup Carrots (Chopped Small)
- 1 cup Carrots (Thinly Sliced)
- 1 cup Baby Corn (Cut in Small Pieces)
- 1 tsp Sesame Seeds
- 1 tsp Black Pepper
- 1 tsp Vinegar
- 1 tbsp Dark Soy Sauce
- 1 tsp Chilli Sauce
- ½ tsp Salt
- 1/4 cup vegetable stock
- 1 cup Green Onion
- 2 tbsp Sunflower Oil

Serves:
2-3 Person

Prep Time:
20 Minutes

Spice Level:
Low

METHOD

- In a wok, fry garlic, ginger and star anise in hot oil for 1 minute.
- Add onions and fry till translucent.
- Then add beans, carrots, cabbage, baby corn and sesame seeds. Fry on high heat for 3-4 minutes.
- Then add rice, all sauces, Vegetable stock, Vinegar, Black pepper, ½ Spring Onion and Salt. Mix it well. Add more Soya Sauce if rice looks a bit dry.
- Now take it out in a large bowl and garnish it with the remaining spring onions. Serve hot.

Sabeen Secrets:

- Rice should be cooked since no cooking will be done during the dish.
- Make sure to not add too much vegetable stock else the rice can get sticky.
- You can also add other vegetables like green peas, bean sprouts and capsicum.

Zeeray Wale Aloo

MAIN

Easy and simple dish from Sabeen's cuisine. It is a classic and hearty Pakistani dish which is slightly spicy yet flavourful.

INGREDIENTS

- 1 kilo Potatoes (Peeled and thinly sliced)
- 2 medium Onion (Finely Chopped)
- 1 ½ tsp Cumin Seeds
- 1 tsp Cumin Powder
- 1 ½ Coriander Powder
- 1 tsp Whole Red Chillies
- 1 tsp Red Chilli
- ¼ tsp Turmeric Powder (Haldi)
- 1 tsp Salt
- 1 tsp Ginger Garlic Paste
- Few Strands of Fresh Coriander (Chopped)
- 1 Green Chilli
- 1 Cup Oil

Serves:
3-4 Person

Prep Time:
45 Minutes

Spice Level:
Low

METHOD

- Soak chopped potatoes in water for 20 minutes.
- Heat oil in a pot and then add onions to sauté.
- Add Cumin Seeds and Whole Red Chillies to fry.
- Then add Potatoes and bhono.
- Add Salt, Haldi, Red Chillies, Coriander Powder, Cumin Powder, Ginger Garlic Paste and bhono again by adding little water in intervals.
- Once done add water, cover the pot and wait till potatoes cook through.
- Once the water has dried up, then bhono a bit again.
- Add green chillies and chopped coriander leaves.

Sabeen Secrets:

- Make sure that potatoes are not mashed. Potatoes should retain their shape in the cooked dish.

Zabardast Lamb Gola Kebabs

MAIN

These succulent kebabs have an exotic taste and tender texture. This is precisely why they are so addictive and Sabeen loved making them for her clients.

INGREDIENTS

- 1 kg Lamb Mince (Keema)
- 3 Bread Slices
- 1 tsp Dry Papaya Powder
- 3 Lemons
- 1 Chopped Coriander
- 4 Green Chilies (chopped)
- 1 tsp Red Chilli Flakes
- 1 tsp Dry Papaya Powder
- 2 tbsp Gram Flour
- 2 tbsp Ginger (Finely Chopped)
- 1 ½ tsp Ginger Garlic Paste
- 1 tsp Salt
- 1 Cup Yoghurt
- 1 tsp Red Chilli
- 1 tsp Black Pepper Corns
- 50 gms Mozzarella Cheese
- 3-4 tbsp Sunflower Oil
- 1 tsp Ghee

Serves:
3-4 Person

Prep Time:
45 Minutes
(After Marination)

Spice Level:
Low

METHOD

- Put all spices, gram flour, cheese, bread and minced meat in a grinder to grind.
- Leave for 2 hours.
- Then form round balls by folding in yoghurt and fry on Oil/Ghee.
- Garnish with freshly chopped coriander, finely chopped onion rings and whole green chilies.
- Once done, smoke the prepared keema with burning coal and cover the frying pan so the smoke remains inside and infuses into the kebabs to give a nice smoky smell.

Sabeen Secrets:

- Serve with Green Raita and Naan.
- Put the burning coal piece in a foil on top of the kebabs and then put a little oil on it before covering the frying pan. This will release the smoke quickly.

Palak (Spinach) Gosht

MAIN

Another staple in Pakistani households; not so much in ours since our son was not very fond of Palak. When using fresh Palak, Sabeen always added a bit of milk to ensure a smoother taste which we found to be quite amusing. But all-in-all, it tastes beautiful!

INGREDIENTS

- 1 kg Lamb with bones
- 2 ½ kg Palak (We suggest frozen spinach since it's convenient)
- 4 Onions (Medium Chopped)
- 3 Tomatoes (Medium Chopped)
- 2 tsp Ginger Garlic Paste
- 1 tsp Salt
- 1 tsp Dried Fenugreek Leaves
- 1 ½ tsp Red Chilli
- 1 tsp Kashmiri Red Chilli
- 1 ½ tsp Coriander Powder
- 1 tsp Cumin Powder
- ½ tsp Turmeric Powder (Haldi)
- ½ tsp Garam Masala Powder
- 1 cup Yoghurt
- 3-4 tbsp Sunflower Oil

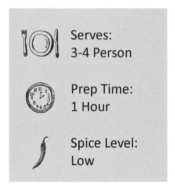

Serves:
3-4 Person

Prep Time:
1 Hour

Spice Level:
Low

METHOD

- Heat Oil in a Pot.
- Add onions and fry until they are light brown in colour.
- Add meat and ginger garlic paste. Fry a little till colour changes.
- Add all spices, tomatoes and bhono (A special way of frying that removes the smell from the meat. Rotate your hand in a circular motion, moving the meat from one side towards the middle of the pot). Adding a little water in intervals. This will stop spices from burning.
- Once the smell of meat is gone, add 3-4 glasses of water and cook on low heat so that meat can become tender.
- Once the meat becomes tender and oil comes on top of the gravy, add yoghurt, fenugreek and bhono.
- Then add Palak and bhono.
- Then cover and put on low heat for 5-7 minutes.
- Add chopped coriander and finely sliced ginger on top to present a colourful dish.

Sabeen Secrets:

- Mix yoghurt well in a cup before adding into the pot.
- Dried fenugreek is a very signature ingredient in Sabeen's cooking. She used to always keep it handy to bring in a special taste.

Chicken Handi (Boneless)

MAIN

Firm favourite for Sabeen in her weekly tiffins. It is quite an effortless dish with tender meat, rich creamy flavour, and mouth-watering aroma. It is usually prepared in a clay pot or traditional small steel karahi.

Serves:
3-4 Person

Prep Time:
45-50 Minutes

Spice Level:
Medium

INGREDIENTS

- 1 kg Chicken breast cut into small pieces (boneless)
- 2 Onions, (Ground)
- 2 Blobs of Butter
- 1 cup Yoghurt
- 1 cup Fresh Cream
- 5-6 Tomatoes (Ground)
- 1 tsp Red Chilli
- 1 tsp Salt
- ½ tsp Turmeric Powder (Haldi)
- ½ tsp Cracked Black Pepper (Grind fresh in the grinder but keep course)
- 1 ½ tsp Kashmiri Red Chilli
- 1 ½ tsp Coriander Powder
- 1 ½ tsp Ginger Garlic Paste
- 1 tsp Cumin Powder
- ¼ tsp Garam Masala
- 1 tsp Dried Fenugreek Leaves
- Finely chopped ginger for garnishing
- 2-3 Green Chillies (Chopped)
- 1/2 bundle of Coriander (Chopped)
- 3-4 tbsp Sunflower Oil

METHOD

- Marinate chicken with yoghurt, all spices, ginger garlic paste and keep aside for 1 hour in the fridge.
- Put Oil and 1 blob of butter in a clay pot and add onion. Then bhono till the smell of the onion is gone.
- Then add marinated chicken and cook.
- Once done, add cream and put on low heat for 10 minutes.
- Finally put a blob of butter on top along with coriander, ginger and green chillies for garnishing.

Sabeen Secrets:

- Cracked black pepper is key to enhancing the taste so make sure that you use freshly crushed black pepper.
- You can pour full cream on the prepared dish to have a rich taste.

Mazedaar
Chicken Chargha

Serves:
2 Person

Prep Time:
1 Hour
(After Marination)

Spice Level:
Medium

SABEEN SIGNATURE/MAIN

A truly signature dish of Sabeen which is extremely easy to make yet still very delicious and fulfilling. This takes you back to Lahore 's Food Streets which is the cultural capital of Pakistan. Serve with hot naan and Sabeen Green Raita.

INGREDIENTS

- 1 kg Whole Chicken (or 12 Chicken Pieces) with Deep Cuts on Skin/Flesh
- 2 tsp Ginger Garlic Paste
- 1 tsp Salt
- 1 tsp Red Chilli
- 1 tsp Cumin Powder
- 1 tsp Coriander Powder
- 1 tsp Cracked Black Pepper
- ½ tsp Turmeric Powder (Haldi)
- 1 tbsp Chat Masala Powder
- Chopped Coriander
- 4 Green Chilies (whole)
- 3-4 tbsp Sunflower Oil
- 1 tsp Ghee

METHOD

- Marinate the chicken with all spices, oil, ghee and ginger garlic paste. Set aside for 3-4 hours.
- Bake marinated chicken in the oven for 45 minutes, at 180 degrees Celsius.
- Once done, cut into four pieces and serve with lemon.
- Add chopped coriander on top to present a colourful dish.

Sabeen Secrets:

- Chicken should remain moist so don't overcook in the oven. Baking also makes chicken dry if overcooked.
- Serve with Sabeen's Green Raita as it enhances the overall experience.

Murgh Zafrani Chicken Curry

Serves:
5-6 Person

Prep Time:
1,5 Hours

Spice Level:
Medium

SABEEN SIGNATURE/MAIN

This is one of the Mughlai Cuisines and makes it a royal dish due to the addition of the most expensive flower in the world; Saffron / Zafran). It has such beautiful aroma and tastes delicious.

INGREDIENTS

- 1 kg Chicken (With Bone)
- 2 Onions (Fried and Crushed)
- 100 gm Tomato Paste
- 5-6 Whole Green Cardamom
- 1 ½ tsp Ginger Garlic Paste
- 1 tsp Salt
- 2 tsp Red Chilli
- 1 tsp Kashmiri Chilli
- 1 tsp Cracked Black Pepper (Grind fresh in the grinder but keep course)

- ½ tsp White Pepper Powder
- 1 ½ tsp Coriander Powder
- 1 cup Yoghurt
- 1 tsp Cumin Powder
- ½ tsp Turmeric Powder (Haldi)
- ¼ tsp Garam Masala Powder
- Few Strands of Zafran (Saffron) mixed in water and left for 2 hours
- 2 Green Chilies (Chopped)
- 3-4 tbsp Sunflower Oil
- 1 tsp Ghee

METHOD

- Marinate chicken with salt, white pepper, ginger garlic paste, garam masala, ½ zafran water (1 tbsp) and mix well. Leave for 60 minutes in the fridge.
- Heat oil and ghee in a pot.
- Add marinated chicken and fry on high flame in 2-3 minutes and then lower flame for 10 minutes till yoghurt dries up.
- Add all spices, whole cardamom and bhono adding a little water in intervals. This will stop spices from burning.
- Once the smell of meat is gone, add 3-4 glasses of water and cook on medium heat for 25-30 minutes till meat is cooked.
- Once the meat is cooked and oil separates, add remaining zafran water, and green chillies. Leave 5 minutes to cook.
- Add chopped coriander and few strands of zafran on top to present a colourful dish.

Sabeen Secrets:

- Make sure chicken meat does not come off the bone while frying.
- Don't overcook the potatoes else it will become a mash.
- Don't wash the mincemeat.

Green Masala Chops

Serves:
4-5 Person

Prep Time:
30 minutes
(After overnight
marination)

Spice Level:
Medium

SABEEN SIGNATURE/MAIN

This dish has succulent texture and intense flavours. The overnight marination infuses strong flavours into the meat to make the taste divine. I remember that in a Chand Raat (Night before Eid) Street Market, a group of guys bought this dish from us and then came afterwards to compliment Sabeen on her awesome cooking. They said it was the perfect chops… Well Done, Sabeen!

INGREDIENTS

- 1 kg Lamb Chops (with fat)
- 1 tsp Lemon Juice
- 1 tsp Salt
- 1 tsp Cracked Black Pepper
- 1 tsp Red Chilli Powder
- 1 ½ tsp Ginger Garlic Paste
- ¼ tsp Garam Masala Powder
- 4 Green Chillies
- 1 bundle Coriander (Roughly Chopped)
- 3-4 strands of Mint (Roughly Chopped)
- 3 Onions (Finely Chopped)
- 3-4 tbsp Sunflower Oil
- 1 tsp Ghee

METHOD

- Put all spices, coriander, lemon juice, onions, green chillies and 1 tbsp water to grind. It should form a thick paste.
- Marinate the chops overnight with this paste.
- Pan-fry the lamb chops till tender and cooked.
- Add chopped coriander on top to present a colourful dish.

Sabeen Secrets:

- Don't overcook the chops as they will become chewy.
- If you don't have time, then just marinate for 1 hour.

Special Desi Lamb Burgers

SNACK

Sabeen created this fusion by combining an English recipe with Desi ingredients. They are juicy, yummy and an absolute Asian treat.

INGREDIENTS

- Lamb mince 1/2 kg (with fat)
- ½ tsp Ginger Garlic Paste
- 1tsp Salt
- 1 tsp Pepper
- 1 tsp Ground Cumin
- ½ tsp Garam masala
- ¼ tsp Ground turmeric
- ½ tsp Cayenne Pepper
- 4 Burger Buns
- 1 Onion (Medium, Thinly Sliced)
- 1 Tomato (Medium, Thinly Sliced)
- 4 Lettuce Leaves

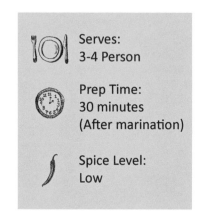

Serves:
3-4 Person

Prep Time:
30 minutes
(After marination)

Spice Level:
Low

METHOD

- Mix ground lamb with all spices and ginger garlic paste. Set aside for 1 hour.
- Divide ground lamb into 4 equally sized patties.
- Sprinkle salt and pepper on both sides.
- Heat a large skillet over medium-high heat.
- Add patty in the skillet and shallow fry till done.
- Spread each top and bottom bun with Sabeen's Special Green Raita.
- Put in the fried patty now and top with tomato, onion rings and lettuce.

HER LOVE Of MARKET STALLS

Sabeen loved doing Street Food markets and was always finding opportunities to display her cooking skills. She was invited by several street food organisers across London and had been part of some really large events where more than 5,000 people visited. She did Festivals, Pubs, Church Street Parties, Street Food Markets, Indoor events, and many others. This was a summer food street market along the River Thames:

The annual Brentford Festival:

View insights

Liked by sabeenkarachicity and 17 others
pinkoveninfo thanks to everyone who came in and told us that the food was amazing! We Sold Out all our food in the Brentford Festival yesterday... more
2 September 2019

Church Market at Isleworth:

Chiswick Food Market (Every Sunday):

And her Favourite: monthly Isleworth Market on South Street

pinkoveninfo   ...

View Insights   Promote

  Liked by **old_isleworth_market** and **7 others**

pinkoveninfo Pink Oven celebrated its 2nd Birthday on the 7th Dec in The Old Isleworth's Christmas Market... more

10 December 2019

pinkoveninfo
London, United Kingdom   ...

View Insights   Promote

Liked by **sabeenkarachicity** and **21 others**

pinkoveninfo Pakoras are the best for the cold rainy winter season. These pics are of our last summer stall in The Old Isleworth Market www.pinkoven.co.uk #london 🇬🇧 #london #londonfood #streetfood #pakistanistreetstyle #asianfood #pakoras #foodporn #food #foodphotography #foodismedicine

YOUR LOCAL FORTNIGHTLY MARKET
— 1ST & 3RD SATURDAY EACH MONTH —

NEXT MARKET

THIS SATURDAY 7 JULY 2018

10AM TO 2PM 📍 SHREWSBURY WALK, ISLEWORTH

Join us for a French themed
market to celebrate
the entente cordiale!

Here are some of her best-selling street food recipes that are sure to take you to the sights and sounds of these markets:

Highway Special Dumba (Lamb) Karahi

SNACK

From the Southern City of Karachi to the Northern city of Peshawar, Karahi is one dish that everyone likes. There are several restaurants located on various highways of Pakistan specialising in Karahis since truckers love this dish as well! They provide traditional Charpais (a traditional woven bed) to make people comfortable on their long journeys. Sabeen had her own take on Karahi using what she called "Cracked Black Pepper". The final dish can be eaten with either Naan or White Rice. It was also a dish in great demand during food festivals and street food markets.

INGREDIENTS

- 1 kg Lamb with bones
- ½ cup Yoghurt
- 7-8 medium Tomatoes (Cut in Half)
- 1 tsp Red Chilli
- 1 tsp Cracked Black Pepper Powder (Grind fresh in grinder but keep course)
- 1 tsp White Pepper Powder
- 1 ½ tsp Kashmiri Red Chilli
- 1 ½ tsp Coriander Powder
- ½ tsp Cardamom Powder
- 1 tsp Cumin Powder

- ½ tsp Garam Masala
- 1 tsp Chat Masala
- 1 ½ tsp Ginger Garlic Paste
- 1 tsp Salt
- 1 tsp Dried Fenugreek Leaves
- 6-8 Green Chillies
- ½ bundle of Coriander (Chopped)
- 1 tsp finely sliced Ginger
- 3-4 tbsp Sunflower Oil
- 1 tbsp Ghee

Serves: 5-6 Person

Prep Time: 1 Hour

Spice Level: Medium

METHOD

- Heat Oil in a Karahi (Special wok used for this dish).
- Add meat, salt and ginger garlic paste. Fry till meat colour changes.
- Add half of the tomatoes, keep on medium heat and cover the pot. When tomatoes become tender, remove tomato skin, crush tomatoes and mix together with meat.
- Now add all spices (except fenugreek) and bhono. Add a little water in intervals as this will stop spices from burning.
- Add Yoghurt, dried fenugreek and bhono.
- Once the smell of meat is gone, add 3-4 glasses of water and cook on low heat so that meat can become tender and is completely cooked.
- Once the meat is cooked and oil comes on top of gravy, add ghee remaining half of tomatoes and green chilies. Cook for further 10-12 minutes till tomatoes are soft and green chilies become tender.
- Add chopped coriander and finely sliced ginger on top to present the dish.

Sabeen Secrets:

- Cracked black pepper is key to enhancing the taste, so make sure that you use freshly crushed black pepper.
- This dish can also be done with chicken but then don't put water in it since chicken gets cooked quite easily when you cover the wok.

Chicken Kata Kat

Serves: 3-4 Person Prep Time: 45 minutes Spice Level: Medium

SABEEN SIGNATURE/MAIN

A true Signature dish of Sabeen that she loved cooking! This was a firm favourite at each and every Pink Oven stall in London! Whether it was food streets, food festivals, pub stalls or church street parties, Sabeen would rock with her Chicken Kata Kat. She has also cooked it LIVE on several occasions on an electric griddle and we had people coming to buy it just from being tempted by the smell. Best served with Naan.

INGREDIENTS

- 1 kg Chicken Boneless Breast (Cut into very small pieces)
- 1 Cup Yoghurt(Whisked)
- 5-6 Tomatoes (Cut in Half)
- 1 tsp Red Chilli
- ½ tsp Black Pepper Powder (Grind fresh in grinder but keep course)
- 1 ½ tsp Kashmiri Red Chilli
- 1 ½ tsp Coriander Powder
- 1 tsp Cumin Powder (Toasted)
- ½ tsp Chilli Flakes
- 1 ½ tsp Ginger Garlic Paste
- 1 tsp Salt
- 1 tsp Dried Fenugreek Leaves
- 5-6 Green Chillies (Chopped)
- 1 bundle of Coriander (Chopped)
- 3-4 tbsp Sunflower Oil
- 1 tbsp Ghee

METHOD

- Heat oil in a large pan and fry chicken till colour changes to white.
- Put in ginger garlic paste and all the spices. Bhono.
- Then put tomatoes and bhono.
- Put whisked yoghurt and bhono.
- Once the meat is done and oil comes on top of gravy, add ghee, coriander, fenugreek and green chilies. Cook for further 5-7 minutes till Green Chilies become a bit tender.
- Add freshly chopped coriander and finely sliced ginger on top to present the dish.

Sabeen Secrets:

- Make sure that you have the right cut chicken breast pieces before cooking. Don't try to break the pieces while cooking otherwise the texture is very flaky.
- Fry on high heat first and then medium heat to cook.

Aloo Gosht (with Gravy/Salan)

MAIN

This was the one dish that all members of our family could eat without any fuss and Sabeen got the most requests to make. Our son loves potatoes so if we put it in anything he will eat it! It is also the most frequently appearing dish on Sabeen's weekly tiffin menu for Pink Oven clients.

INGREDIENTS

- 1 kg Lamb with bones
- 6 Onions (Finely Chopped)
- 2 Medium Potatoes (Medium Chopped)
- 4-5 Tomatoes (Medium Chopped)
- 1 ½ tsp Ginger Garlic Paste
- 1 tsp Salt
- 2 tsp Red Chilli
- 1 ½ tsp Coriander Powder
- 1 tsp Cumin Powder
- ½ tsp Turmeric Powder (Haldi)
- ¼ tsp Garam Masala Powder
- Chopped Coriander
- 4 Green Chilies (whole)
- 3-4 tbsp Sunflower Oil
- 1 tsp Ghee

Serves: 5-6 Person

Prep Time: 1 Hour

Spice Level: Medium

METHOD

- Heat oil in a Pot.
- Add onions and fry till brown. It's very important to make sure that onions are completely brown since it helps in making the gravy later on.
- Add meat and ginger garlic paste. Fry a little till colour changes.
- Add tomatoes and bhono (special way of frying that removes the smell from the meat. Rotate your hand in circular motion, moving the meat from one side towards the middle of the pot).
- Add all spices and bhono adding a little water in intervals. This will stop spices from burning.
- Once the smell of meat is gone, add 3-4 glasses of water and cook on low heat so that meat can become tender.
- Once the meat become tender, add potatoes and cook till oil separates from gravy.
- Add green chillies and garam masala. Leave 5 minutes to cook.
- Turn off the heat once potatoes are done.
- Make sure there is enough gravy in the dish as this is supposed to have a good amount of gravy.
- Add chopped coriander on top to present a colourful dish.

Sabeen Secrets:

- Don't chop the potatoes too small.
- Don't overcook the potatoes else it will become a mash.
- If you feel gravy is less, add some water and cook on low heat till it thickens.

Tandoori Chicken

MAIN

Sabeen's Tandoori Chicken is delicious and mouth-watering. I loved this dish since it was without sauce but still oozing with taste. Another regular dish in Weekly Tiffins and London Market Stalls.

INGREDIENTS

- 1 kg Chicken with skin, cut into 10 pieces (with bone and deep bar be cue cuts)
- 1 Onion (Chopped in Fine Slices for Garnishing)
- 1 Blob of Butter
- 1 Cup Yoghurt
- 1 tsp Red Chilli
- 1 tsp Salt
- ½ tsp Turmeric Powder (Haldi)
- 1 tsp Cracked Black Pepper (Grind fresh in grinder but keep course)
- 1 ½ tsp Kashmiri Red Chilli
- 1 ½ tsp Coriander Powder
- 1 ½ tsp Ginger Garlic Paste
- 1 tsp Cumin Powder
- ¼ tsp Garam Masala
- 1 tsp Chat Masala
- 1 tsp Crushed Red Chilli
- Finely chopped Ginger for garnishing
- 2-3 Green Chillies (Chopped)
- 1/2 bundle of Coriander (Chopped)
- 1 tbsp Sunflower Oil
- 1 piece of Coal for Smokey taste

Serves: 3-4 Person

Prep Time: 1 Hour

Spice Level: High

METHOD

- Marinate chicken with yogurt, butter, oil, all spices, ginger garlic paste and keep aside for 2 hours in fridge.
- Arrange chicken on a tray and put in a heated oven at 180 degrees Celsius for 45 minutes.
- Once done, smoke the prepared chicken with burning coal by pouring little oil on top of the coal and covering the tray so the smoke remains inside and infuses into the meat to give nice smoky smell.
- Garnish with coriander, onion, ginger and green chillies.

Sabeen Secrets:

- Make sure to cover the chicken with a foil after 20 minutes so that it does not burn from the top.
- Also check that the chicken is thoroughly cooked.

PESHAWARI LAMB CHAPLI KEBABS

MAIN

Peshawar is the capital of North West Frontier Province, which changed its name to Khyber Pakhtunkhwa (also known as KPK) in 2010. People of KPK are very hard working and they need rich food to get their energy. Chapli Kebabs represent the true spirit of the people of Peshawar and the name comes from the word *Chaprikh* in Pashto meaning flat.

This was one of Sabeen's favourite dishes and also a favourite among patrons of Pink Oven market stalls across London. Best served with hot naan.

INGREDIENTS

- 1 kg Minced Meat (Lamb)
- ¾ cup Animal Fat/Charbee
- ½ tbsp Cumin Powder
- 1 tsp Black Pepper Powder
- ½ tsp Ajwain
- 1 ½ tsp Crushed Dried Red Chilli
- 1 tsp Garam Masala
- 1 ½ tsp Pomegranate Seeds
- 1 cup Gram Flour (Besin)
- 1 ½ tsp Salt
- 1 Chopped Onion (Finely Chopped)
- 1 whole bundle of Chopped Coriander
- 3 medium Tomatoes (Finely chopped)
- 4 Green Chilies (Finely Chopped)
- 2 Tomatoes (Finely sliced in round shapes)
- 2 Eggs
- ½ Cup Sunflower Oil
- 1 Cup Ghee

 Serves: 5-6 Person

 Prep Time: 1 Hour

 Spice Level: High

METHOD

- Take a wide pot/deep pan and put in minced meat along with animal fat and all spices as well as fresh vegetables.
- Make sure to roast the whole dried coriander, cumin and ajwain for 2 minutes, crush it and then add to the minced meat.
- Use your hands to mix together. Keep mixing with your hands and through your fingers till it turns into a very smooth texture. This will take a bit of time so don't rush it.
- Then add 2 eggs, oil and mix again.
- Leave it for 30 minutes to set.
- After 30 minutes heat enough Ghee in the frying pan to submerge the kebabs.
- Then make flat kebab patty, put one slice of tomato on the top of kebab, push in a bit and fry in Ghee till done on both sides.

Sabeen Secrets:

- Put some oil on your palms when making the patty.
- Put the kebab patty on baking paper so it does not stick and will be easier to handle before frying.
- Don't over fry the kebab since it will make the outer layer hard.

Mashoor Punjabi Cholay

MAIN

This dish is very famous (Mashoor) in the Punjab province of Pakistan and especially in the provincial capital of Lahore. It was in demand in our market stalls due to Sabeen's recipe which gave it creamy texture and heavenly taste. Customers fell in love with it, although we seldom had it in home. Eat with Naan, rice or even on its own with a spoon.

INGREDIENTS

- 500 gm Boiled Chickpeas
- 1 Onion (Pureed)
- 1 ½ tsp Ginger Garlic Paste
- 1 tsp Salt
- 1 tsp Cumin Seeds
- 1 tsp Red Chilli
- 1 tsp Cumin Powder
- 1 tsp Dry Kasoori Methi

- 1 ½ tsp Coriander Powder
- ½ tsp Turmeric Powder (Haldi)
- ¼ tsp Garam Masala Powder
- ¼ Bundle Chopped Coriander
- 1 Green Chilli (Chopped)
- 1 tbsp Sunflower Oil
- 3 tbsp Ghee
- 2 Blobs of Butter (Approx. 100 gm)

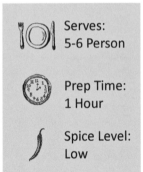

Serves:
5-6 Person

Prep Time:
1 Hour

Spice Level:
Low

METHOD

- Heat ghee in a pot.
- Add ginger garlic paste and fry by adding a little water.
- Add cumin seeds and fry. Then add onion puree and fry till light brown.
- Add all spices (except garam masala and fenugreek) and bhono by adding little water in intervals.
- Then add chickpeas and bhono for 5 minutes. Then add 2-3 cups of water and cover the lid for 20 minutes till chickpeas become soft.
- Now add garam masala and fenugreek and cover for 3-4 minutes.
- Finally add butter and coriander to mix.
- Add chopped coriander and green chillies on top to present a colourful dish.

Sabeen Secrets:

- Sabeen always added butter to make the texture creamy. This was her secret.

Lamb Afghani Pulao (Sabeen Style)

MAIN

I preferred Biryani over Pulao until I started eating Sabeen's Afghani Pulao after we got married. The dish has lamb falling off the bones, is flavourful from the carrots and raisins and has so much aromatic flavour that no one can resist. It was also a bestselling item at her London Market Stalls.

INGREDIENTS

- 1 kg Lamb cut in small pieces (with bone)
- ½ cup Raisins
- 1 kg Rice (4 Cups)
- 3 Onions, Medium Chopped
- 500 gms Carrot (Finely Grated)
- 1 cup Yoghurt
- 5-6 Tomatoes (grinded)
- 1 tsp Red Chilli
- 1 tsp Salt
- 1 tsp Turmeric Powder (Haldi)
- 1 tsp Cracked Black Pepper (Grind fresh in grinder but keep course)
- 1 ½ tsp Coriander Powder
- 1 tsp Cumin Powder
- 1 ½ tsp Ginger Garlic Paste
- 3-4 tbsp Sunflower Oil
- 1 tbsp Ghee

 Serves: 4-5 Person

 Prep Time: 1.5 hours

 Spice Level: Low

METHOD

- Fry lamb with salt in oil and ghee and take out once colour changes.
- Add carrot in same pot, fry for 2-3 minutes and take out.
- Now fry onion till golden brown.
- Then add whole garam masala, lamb and fry. Add ginger garlic paste and all spices. Bhono by adding little water in intervals till oil comes up.
- Then add 8 cups of water to cook since rice will have to be added to this mix as well.
- Soak rice in water for 10 minutes and once water in pot is boiling, add the rice.
- Once rice absorbs the water, then put fried onion, carrots, raisins and put on dum for 20 minutes.
- Once rice is cooked, lift from the sides with a flat spoon bringing it towards the centre. This will help mix the rice nicely with all the ingredients.

Sabeen Secrets:

- Make sure that rice does not overcook, so balance of water and rice needs to be perfect.

Special Tarka Daal

MAIN

Daal is a staple for Pakistani households and is something that people cook to take a break from meat! Sabeen always served it with her special Tarka so it looked good as well as being appetising. Goes well with Achar, Papar and White Rice.

INGREDIENTS

- 500 gms Red Lentils (Masoor Daal)
- 2-3 Tomatoes (Medium Diced)
- 1 ½ tsp Ginger Garlic Paste
- ¼ tsp Turmeric Powder (Haldi)
- ¾ tsp Red Chilli Powder
- 1 ½ tsp Coriander Powder
- Salt to taste

Serves:
4-5 Person

Prep Time:
1.5 hours

Spice Level:
Low

METHOD

- Wash Red Lentils thoroughly to remove all dirt.
- Put oil and fry the washed lentils for few minutes.
- Then add 2-3 cups of water along with all the spices, diced tomatoes and ginger garlic paste.
- Put on medium heat and cook till lentils are tender.
- Then take a blender or manually press the contents of the pot so the lentils become smooth and runny in texture.

Tarka Prep:

- Add 1 tsp whole cumin, whole red chilli, diced garlic and curry leaves to hot ghee.
- Fry for few minutes making sure that it does not burn.
- Add on top of the cooked lentils so that it makes a sizzling sound.
- Enjoy Special Tarka Daal.

Sabeen Secrets:

- Sprinkle lemon on top before eating to enhance the taste.

Peri Peri Wings

MAIN

Simple yet extremely delicious. We used to have this at lunch when there was no appetite for heavy main meals. You can have it with Sabeen's Green Raita. Sabeen has also served this regularly in our Market Stalls and Client Parties.

INGREDIENTS

- 1 kg Chicken wings (Washed and Drained)
- 4 Red Chillies (Mexican Cereno Chillies)
- 3 Garlic Bulbs
- ½ bundle Parsley
- 1 tbsp Smoked Paprika
- 1 tsp Dried Oregano
- 1 tsp Salt
- 1 tbsp Lemon Juice
- 1 tbsp Olive Oil

 Serves:
4-5 Person

 Prep Time:
1 Hours

 Spice Level:
Medium

METHOD

- Blend all ingredients along with oil.
- Marinate wings and leave for 30 minutes.
- To cook the wings, you can bake or grill them.
- Heat oven at 180 degrees Celsius. Put the wings on butter paper in a tray and bake for 40 minutes. Halfway change the side to give even colour on both sides.

PASSION AND
COMPASSION

While Sabeen loved Pink Oven and her entrepreneurial success, she was also full of compassion for the people around her. She liked helping people on the streets, in her friendship circles and even her clients.

There are many people who confided in her and wanted to share their personal situations with her. She always listened with patience and gave them her thoughts.

My maternal uncle and his family had a stopover for one night in Dubai while travelling to Pakistan from Toronto. Sabeen was 7 months pregnant with Sameer at that time and we were living in our one-bedroom apartment. She still insisted on sleeping on the sofa to give her bed up for my uncle's family so they could have a good night's sleep. I hope they remember and appreciated that!

Here are some recipes that show her passion for her skills and innovation:

Karachi Style Anday Walay Bun Kabab

MAIN

One of the most loved street foods in Pakistan. This is very nostalgic for millions of Pakistani diasporas and getting it right to the taste of Karachiite's is not an easy task. Sabeen was always looking to offer something new to her Pink Oven clients and thus came her Bun Kabab recipe.

INGREDIENTS

- 1 cup Chana Dal(Soaked Overnight)
- 3 Large Potatoes
- 10 Pieces Whole Red Chilies
- 1 tbsp Cumin Seeds
- 1/2 tsp Garam Masala
- 1 tsp Chat Masala
- 1 tsp Salt
- 1 Medium Onion (Very Finely Chopped, Round Fine Strands)
- Ginger Garlic Paste 1 tsp
- Round Buns (Brioche is Better)
- Eggs 3 beaten

Sabeen's Green Chutney:

- 1 tbsp Chopper Coriender
- 1 tsp Chopper Mint
- 1 tsp Sugar
- ½ tsp Salt
- 1 tsp Black Pepper
- Grind all ingredients with 2 tbsp of water to make a slightly thick paste. Should not be too thick.

Serves:
3-4 Person

Prep Time:
1 hour
(After Soaking Dal)

Spice Level:
Medium

METHOD

- In a pot, boil potatoes till soft. Discard the water and mash the potatoes.
- In a separate pan add chana daal, whole red chilies, cumin seeds and 4 cups water boil it until all the liquid dries. Keep checking as the dal should not lose its shape but should be soft when pressed.
- Let the daal mixture cool a bit and then grind adding salt, chat masala and garam masala and keep it in a bowl. Then add the mashed potatoes to the daal mixture and mix well.
- Now beat the eggs and make round patty with the mixture. In a frying pan heat the oil, dip in the beaten eggs and shallow fry both sides till golden brown.
- Now fry the remaining eggs and keep it aside. Now heat the pan and warm the buns with little oil.
- It's time to assemble the bun kababs. Spread Sabeen's Green Chutney at the bottom, then put fried egg and potato patty on top.
- Spread ketchup on top and put onions. Put the other half of the bun on top and serve with fries.

Masaledar Full Lamb Leg Roast

 Serves:
4-5 Person

 Prep Time:
2 Hours

Spice Level:
Medium

MAIN

This was a firm Eid favourite in our house as well as among Sabeen's clients. We used to either bar-b-que or put it in the oven to cook thoroughly. Meat is succulent and tender, infused with Pakistani spices which makes it a whole new experience.

INGREDIENTS

- 1 Whole Lamb Leg with Fat (Put Deep Cuts, but not too deep)
- ½ kg Baby Potatoes (Cut in Half)
- 1 cup Yoghurt
- 500 gms Frozen Peas
- 4 cups Basmati Rice (1 kg)
- 1 ½ tbsp Coriander Powder
- 1 tbsp Cumin Powder
- 1 tbsp Red Chilli
- 1 tbsp Garam Masala Powder
- 1 tbsp White Pepper
- 1 tbsp Cracked Black Pepper
- 1 tbsp Salt
- 1 tbsp Meat Tenderizer
- 1 tbsp Crushed Red Chilli
- 1 tbsp Turmeric (Haldi)
- 2 tbsp Ginger Garlic Paste
- ½ tbsp Cardamom Powder
- ½ tsp Jaifal (Nutmeg Powder)
- ½ tsp Javatri (Mace Powder)
- 1 tbsp Lemon Juice
- 6-7 Whole Green Chillies
- 1 Large Lemon (Cut in Fine Slices)
- 3-4 tbsp Oil

METHOD

- Mix all ingredients together along with oil. It should form a paste.
- Apply the paste to the lamb leg and rub well. Fill inside the cuts so that the flavours can infuse inside the meat. Leave overnight in the fridge to marinate.
- Now take a large pot (you can also use a steamer) and place the marinated meat. Place green chillies and lemon slices on top along with the excess masala paste. Now cover the pot and let it steam for 45 minutes on low heat.
- After 30 minutes, turn over the leg piece, pour more masala paste/sauce from the pot on top (repeat 3-4 times) and leave it again for 45 minutes.
- If the meat is done, then fry it by adding 1 cup oil for 10 minutes.
- Then place it in oven at 160 degrees Celsius for another 20-25 minutes. This will lock in all the flavours and the masala will stick to the meat.
- Now add boiled potatoes in the same pot and fry till all masala is coated on the potatoes.
- Also boil the rice and add butter when giving dum.
- Once meat is done, take out in an Arabic Thaal (Large Round Steel Dish) layer first with rice, put roasted leg on top and spread the fried potatoes and peas around the leg.

PINKOVENINFO
Posts

pinkoveninfo   ...

View Insights   Promote

Liked by **madiha.siddiqui.5** and **8 others**
pinkoveninfo Succulent Lamb Roast with Potatoes
and Peas made by Pink Oven made on order
3 January 2018

pinkoveninfo   ...

Sabeen Secrets:

- Don't make the cuts too deep else the whole leg will lose its shape.
- Sabeen used to serve whole, peeled and boiled potatoes with it. These were dipped and fried in the excess masala paste to give it flavour.
- You can serve with basmati butter rice.

Chilli Achari Paneer

Serves: 3-4 Person

Prep Time: 1 Hour

Spice Level: High

SABEEN SIGNATURE/MAIN

Loved this dish from Sabeen; it is my personal favourite. The Paneer cooked in spicy flavours makes your palate come alive. Must try!

INGREDIENTS

- 500 gm Paneer (Cottage Cheese)
- 6 Whole Red Chillies
- 2 tbsp Coriander Seeds
- 2 tbsp Fennel Seeds
- 2 tbsp Cumin Seeds
- 1 ½ tbsp Mustard Seeds
- ½ tsp Fenugreek Seeds
- 1 ½ tsp Kalonji (Nigella Seeds)
- 2 Tomatoes (Medium Chopped)
- 1 Capsicum (Medium Chopped)
- 1 ½ tsp Ginger Garlic Paste
- 1 tsp Green Chilli Paste
- ¾ tsp Turmeric Powder (Haldi)
- 1 tsp Salt
- 1 tsp Kashmiri Red Chilli Powder
- 1 ½ Cup Yoghurt(Whisked)
- ½ Bundle Chopped coriander
- 4 Green Chilies (whole)
- 3-4 tbsp Sunflower Oil
- 1 tsp Ghee

METHOD

- Roast whole red chillies, coriander seeds, fennel seeds, cumin seeds, mustard seeds and fenugreek seeds in a pan for 1-2 minutes. Then cool this spice mixture and grind to keep aside. This is your Achari masala.
- Now chop capsicum and tomatoes in medium size. Then blend these together to form a paste. Keep aside.
- Heat ghee and oil in a pot and add kalonji. Fry for 1-2 minutes on medium heat and then add ginger garlic paste and green chilli paste to sauté for 1 minute.
- Add haldi, Kashmiri red chilli and a little water to bhono for few seconds
- Now add tomato and capsicum puree and bhono.
- Add Achari masala mix and salt, bhono for 3-4 minutes.
- Then add whisked yogurt and bhono till it boils.
- Add paneer and mix well with the gravy. Let it cook for 10 minutes.
- Add chopped coriander, green chillies on top to present a colourful dish.

Sabeen Secrets:

- You can also fry the paneer before putting it in the gravy.
- The gravy should be thick and not runny.

HER FINAL CHAPTER

With the emergence of Covid-19 at the end of 2019 and its explosion in 2020, Sabeen was quite worried. Sabeen had Asthma and High Blood Pressure, so she was very careful to avoid contracting it. We were also shielding her as much as possible and she had not been to a grocery store for months. Still with all these precautions and the decision to re-open schools, Sabeen contracted Covid-19 in December 2020 and had to be admitted to hospital on 6 Jan 2021. After a couple of days, the doctors decided that she would need a ventilator to recover, and she was put on one on 8th of January. Her doctors were confident that she would recover and none of us imagined that she would never recover. She eventually passed away on the 24th of February 2021 after fighting for her life for 7 weeks. All our family and friends kept praying for her for these 7 weeks, but Allah had a different plan.

It was a terrible and tragic event in our lives; we loved Sabeen with all our hearts and we never imagined life without her. She was the centre of our attention and care. We always protected her from all harm, but Covid is ruthless, and it eventually got to her. We are incomplete without her and mourn her death every day; the mention of her name is enough for tears to roll down my face. She was a truly special person, who was innocent, intelligent and loved by all the people around her. We had the best married life a couple could ever have. We lived like friends and were very happy as a family.

Her funeral was on the 26th of February, and I managed everything with the help of my best friend Yasir Sheikh. It was very difficult to see her in the casket, cover her face and then put her in the grave; but I knew that Sabeen would have wanted her loving husband to do it for her. I was fortunate enough to spend my life with her for 25 years and lucky to do all her last rites with my own hands. The funeral was attended by a few members of my family, friends and office colleagues who came with zeal as they felt heart broken by Sabeen's untimely departure.

We still cannot believe that she is gone, and we will never be able to see her and speak to her again. The loss of a loved one is the worst kind of emotional pain. Lots of people advise you to accept it but will never know how difficult it is to accept.
After her sad demise, people who only interacted with her on social media were also remembering her professionalism and kindness. Her clients were shocked and very sad, offering us their help and support.

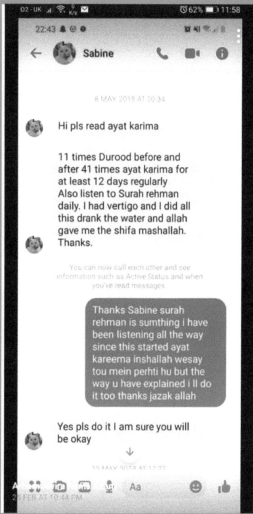

I am really sorry for your loss.

I was always so impressed by Sabeen's hard work, dedication and even her kindness.

I realized that everyone she has interacted with has felt the same and I pray that this is sadaqah jariah for her, the kindness with which she has touched so many lives.

Praying for you and your son, and the rest of the family, to find solace at this time.

19:30

Thu 11 Mar

Naz Naz Khan
Inna lillahi wa inna ilayhi rajioon. May Allah SWT grant her a place in jannah and accept her without any questioning. I remember this lady starting her business and I was so impressed with her flavours. Just shows how short life is 😞😞

The best one was from a client who had her baby's birth catered by Sabeen:

"Last night I found out that Sabine Mans of @pink oven passed away due to Covid. She was a young, lovely, polite, sweet, ambitious woman. She catered the event for my son's welcome party. She came highly recommended, so I thought ok let's give her a try. Waqar and I are super picky and snooty when it comes to food taste. Her food was loved by everyone in attendance. Sabine had shown my postpartum deranged, party planning odd mommy so much love. As usual, I had planned this event last minute, as usual with my indecisiveness I changed the menu ten times, i asked a million questions, i second guessed everything and she listened, answered, suggested, helped all through serious amounts of patience.

We followed each other on insta, on Facebook. She would comment on my stories every now she and then especially about ayyAd. I ordered some food again from her last year and it has been a while since we talked. I had no idea she was ill with covid. I had no idea she was critical... I only found out yesterday that she passed away.

The pink oven was her dream child built by both her, and her hubby and their son was an equal part of their venture. Throughout my event, the 3 of them were there working tirelessly, providing the best customer care possible. I cannot imagine the personal loss these two must be feeling.

I've not been able to sleep since last night, I keep thinking about her, i even saw her in my dream. I've only met her once, but because I've had this connection with her through my son. My first ever event for him, made memorable and beautiful by her work, my heart grieves. I had a chat with her about her business and how she started, and it was absolutely an amazing story. I told her, one day iA we will sit and discuss this in detail but that one day didn't happen... Her legacy is her business and her child.. I pray to Allah that the kind of patience, love and sweetness she showed me when planning the event, that Allah allows her 70 times more than that as she has now begun the journey to her next life."

We also celebrated her birthday, which happened a short while after her passing away on the 9th of March. On her last birthday, Sabeen asked us to have her next cake made by her friend who is a professional cake decorator. I contacted her and she made a truly special cake that we cut to celebrate her birthday.

Her close friends were inconsolable on her birthday:

We were immensely supported by our family and my office friends/colleague as well as Sameer's friends. Everyone rallied around us and gave us the support we needed, although the pain never went away. My office also sent us a beautifully designed Condolence Book which was signed by people all over the globe.

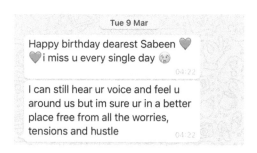

> **Tue 9 Mar**
>
> Happy birthday dearest Sabeen 🤍 🤍 i miss u every single day 🐾
> 04:22
>
> I can still hear ur voice and feel u around us but im sure ur in a better place free from all the worries, tensions and hustle
> 04:22

Happy Birthday in Heaven

I miss you like anything

We finally include her most loved recipe that is simple to make and is most commonly served in Pakistani Funerals as comfort food.

Words can't describe the amount of pain that I've been feeling since you've left, but it's not even just me, it's everyone. Happy Birthday Sabeen 🤍

SHAHI KHEER (RICE PUDDING)

Serves:
4 Person

Prep Time:
30-40 minutes

Sabeen Signature/Dessert

This is my personal favourite. The creamy texture of the rice pudding that Sabeen created along with finely grounded nuts, royal touch of the edible silver leaf and aroma of edible rose petals gives a heavenly experience. Yum!

INGREDIENTS

- 4 cups or 1L Whole Milk
- 400 gm Boiled Rice
- ½ Cup Sugar
- ½ Cup Condensed Milk
- ¼ tsp Cardamom Powder
- 2 tbsp Pistachio (Finely Chopped)
- 2 tbsp Almond (Finely Chopped)
- 1 tsp Rose Water
- 1-2 Silver Leaf
- 1 tsp Dried Rose Petals

METHOD

- Heat milk in the pot.
- Once milk is hot (but not boiling), add sugar in it and mix well.
- Then add cardamom powder and keep stirring.
- Once it starts to boil a bit, add rice. Keep stirring till the mixture becomes thick.
- Then add condensed milk and keep stirring.
- Then add almonds and pistachio. Keep some for garnishing later. Keep stirring for 10 minutes and switch off the flame.
- Garnish with remaining almonds and pistachio.
- Then delicately put the silver leaf on top and spread the rose petals around it.

Sabeen Secrets:

- You can also fry the paneer before putting it in the gravy.
- The gravy should be thick and not runny.

HER LEGACY CONTINUES

After the funeral, we felt lost and did not know how to handle our lives. Still today we are struggling; but the one thing that we were sure of is to continue her legacy with Pink Oven. My son decided that the best way to honour his Mum was to not let her business die out as well.

Sameer has always been interested in hospitality and catering; he has a distinction in this subject from school and like his mother has a keen interest in cooking. This has served as a blessing since now Sameer has taken over cooking food for Pink Oven with my support. This has enabled us to continue the various business streams, Tiffin's, Parties, Corporate Events and Market Stalls. We have relaunched the business successfully with clients supporting our decision.

Aslamoalikum Mansoor,

You are doing a great thing by continuing Sabeen's legacy. She worked too hard for the whole setup to just be forgotten. Well done! We can imagine how hard it must be for you but with time inshallah things will fall into place and get easier. 18:31

Yes it's very hard....we miss Sabeen every moment of our lives ... she was a kind, humble, loving and beautiful person. If you had met her you would have really liked her. And thus we wanted to continue her legacy and passion. 18:33

We are also continuing Market Stalls as Sabeen enjoyed being part of them. She loved the live interaction with her customers and to share her delicious cuisine with a variety of people.

We also decided to write this book since we wanted to keep her name alive. We strongly believe that by sharing her passion and compassion widely, we will succeed in communicating the importance of ambition, love for the family and empathy towards people. We don't only consider this book to be a celebration of Sabeen's beautiful life but also of her values which she has passed on to us – and we hope through her recipes and stories, they will be passed on to you too. This gives us purpose and reason to continue living.

One day we will also fulfil her dream of opening a restaurant: Pink Oven by Sabeen. This will complete all her dreams and fill us with the happiness that we have lost for now.

A WORD FROM HER SISTER

I was asked to write a short eulogy for my sister Sabeen.

It's not easy and I don't have words to express how much I miss her each and every day. I was always overprotective for Sabeen during our school years as girls used to bully her. She was so quiet, so I used to stand up for her.

We loved playing practical jokes and nobody including our teachers and my parents' friends were spared. We would spend time making elaborate plans on how to conduct the prank; and every time it was a success!

We spent hours talking on the phone recently and remember our childhood memories. Now I don't have anyone to share those memories.

A few days before getting sick Sabeen called me one day and said that we should have a sisters' vacation and travel to Dubai as we haven't spent much time together recently. I was so excited but never knew that the last time I saw her a decade ago was the final goodbye.

I miss you Sabeen very much!

Apa

A WORD fROM HER MOTHER

The doctor held her up for me to see......a sweet little bundle of joy!! Loving and caring. What else could she be!? Her name meant FAMILY, and that her husband and son, were very close to her heart.

She was an excellent and loving mother and groomed her son according to her high values and principles of life.

Sabeen had a kind nature and was an animal lover. She took in a stray cat and pampered her like a mama! Even in hospital, before going on the ventilator, she was thinking of Sky.

Her purity of heart and innocence left a mark on those who touched her life.
What a girl! What a shining star.

We all miss her.

Allah please take special care of my baby.

May she rest in peace.

Love you always,

Ami

A WORD FROM HER MOTHER -IN-LAW

My Dearest Daughter Sabeen,

I still remember the day when we met you for the first time and told your mother that from now on, Sabeen is our daughter. You made a deep place in our hearts with your kind and nice nature. Usually there are problems in the relationship of daughters-in-law and mother-in-law but in all these years, we never had any problems. You always remained nice to us and happy with us. Our hearts explode when we think now that you are not with us anymore! I am in a lot of pain to face the fact that you left us so early; we never thought that we will face this day.

We think of you every moment, we pray for you every day. May Allah gives you the highest place in Heaven. Ameen.

I still remember the days we spent together in Dubai where you cooked such delicious food for us as well as your ever smiling face. But this is the will of Allah and we cannot do anything. Allah has given you the status of Martyr which everyone does not get. Probably that's why Allah has called you back early.

You were the dignity, radiance, and happiness of our house....and will always be.

Love,
Your Aunty.

A WORD FROM HER SISTER IN LAWS

To our beloved Sister-in- law,

Never in a million years had we ever thought that we would be writing a tribute in your loving memory. You came into our lives and instantly became part of it, you accepted us with an open heart and so much love. We loved talking to you as it was always so much fun, we miss your laugh terribly. Our hearts ache as we pen down our emotions and feelings for you as we still can't believe you are not there with us anymore.

You were the most sweet and humble person, a beautiful woman inside out, a great wife and an amazing mother. We were so lucky to have you as our sister-in-law and got to spend so many beautiful years with you. When we met last time we had such great time shopping, having food together, we still remember those scrumptious Chapli kababs that you made for us, and you made us laugh so hard that we almost cried, little did we know that we won't get to see you again.

Every day we ask this question to ourselves that why you? Why has Allah taken you from us so soon? We miss you every day. You have left a void in our hearts that can never be filled for the rest of our lives. None of our occasions or happy moments will ever be complete now. To sum up our love for you in few words is very difficult because you were more than just a sister-in-law for us you were a friend a sister a confidant, Sabeen you hold a very very special place in our hearts.

You are in a wonderful place now, a place where you had always belonged to 'Heaven'. May Allah rest your soul in peace Ameen.

Love you Bhabhi….Till we meet again..

9.March - 24.February.2021

Mona & Madiha

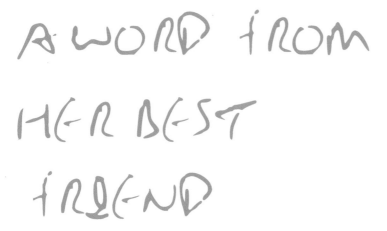

A WORD FROM HER BEST FRIEND

My beloved friend Sabeen.

I still cannot believe that you are no longer with us. I keep on praying that may Allah grant you highest place in Jannah. Ameen.

I still remember the first time we met back in 1993 and instantly became friends and thankfully that friendship stood the test of time. I miss your pranks and your joyous laughter and especially how you used to keep on reminding me of your birthday again and again as soon as march began. 9th March will never be the same without you here with me.

I am so happy that you and Mansoor brought up Sameer to be such an amazing young man who will carry your legacy forward. Mansoor is an amazing husband and father. Alhamdulillah.

 I pray that may Allah unite you with your family in Jannah.

Ameen Summa Ameen

Sabeen Ashraf

A WORD FROM HER CLOSE FRIEND

Dear Sabeen,

My life was blessed through your friendship. You'll never be forgotten that simply cannot be. As long as I am living, I'll carry you with me in my heart.

I love you every day. And now I will miss you every day and this is how I always remember you.

May you be as blessed in the next life.

Maria

HUSBAND

TRIBUTE

تو بدن میں ہوں سایا
تو نہ ہو تو میں کہاں ہوں
مجھے پیار کرنے والے
تو جہاں ہے میں وہاں ہوں

You are the body, I am the shadow
Without you I don't exist
Oh, you who love me
I am only there where you are

YOUR LOVE AND HUSBAND

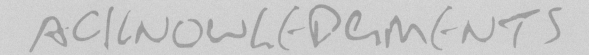

ACKNOWLEDGMENTS

Thank you to the lovely people who have joined us in making this cookbook possible. We are so very grateful to your dedication.

Sue Phillips, Isabelle Rowan, Kristina Boikova, Lucy Neiland, Madiha Fahad, Maimona Shafiq and Humaira Shafiq.

FINALLY, WE OWE A HUGE DEBT OF THANKS TO BILLIE ING WHO WORKED TIRELESSLY AND PASSIONATELY TO LEAD THE EFFORT ON THIS BOOK. SHE MARSHALLED THE TEAM, REVIEWED THE CONTENT, GUIDED ON THE STORY AS WELL AS PROVIDED MORAL SUPPORT TO OUR FAMILY.

WITHOUT YOUR HELP, THIS WOULD NOT HAVE BEEN POSSIBLE.

I KNOW SABEEN

Born on: 9 March 1977

Favourite Country: UK

Favourite City: London

Favourite Chocolate: Lion & After Eight

Favourite Crisps: Lays Max Hot Chicken Wings Flavour

Favourite Vacation Destination: Paris

Favourite Song: I am Levitating (Dua Lipa) & Careless Whisper (George Michael)

Favourite International Chef: Ina Garten

Favourite Pakistani Cook: Samina Jalil

Favourite Color: Pink

Favourite Flower: Lavender

Favourite pass time: Pakistani Dramas & Food Videos

Favourite Writer: Danelle Steel

Favourite Channel: Hum Masala TV

Love of her life: Me :(

Favourite Ice Cream: NUII

She used to call me: Mansi

OUR LIFE IN PICTURES

WE LOVE SABEEN

Sabeen Mansoor.

Lightning Source UK Ltd.
Milton Keynes UK
UKHW050658060921
389976UK00003B/40